A TASTE OF LUCCA

A TASTE OF LUCCA

Hosting a
Northern Italian
Dinner Party

Recipes · Menus · Planning · Wines · Entertaining

by Deborah Dinelli

TZEDAKAH PUBLICATIONS

A Taste of Lucca:
Hosting a Northern Italian Dinner Party

For information, address
Tzedakah Publications, P.O. Box 221097
Sacramento, CA 95822

Cover and text design and illustration by
Lisa Bacchini Graphic Design and Illustration

Library of Congress Cataloging-in-Publication Data

Dinelli, Deborah, 1955–
    A taste of Lucca: hosting a Northern Italian dinner party: recipes, menus, planning, wines, entertaining / by Deborah Dinelli — 1st ed.
        p. cm.
    Includes index.
    ISBN 0-929999-07-X : $14.95
    1. Cookery, Italian—Northern style. 2. Cookery—Italy—Lucca. 3. Menus. 4. Dinners and dining. I. Title.

    TX723.2.N65D56 1994   94-17315
    641.5945'5—dc20   CIP

ISBN 0-929999-07-X

FIRST EDITION
10 9 8 7 6 5 4 3 2 1

This cookbook is dedicated to my mother, Annie Dinelli,
without whose wonderful cooking this book would not have been possible.

ACKNOWLEDGMENTS

I want to thank the following people for their help and support with my cookbook:
Francesco "Cecco" Manfredini, who helped me so much with the proverbs, special stories of the past
and details about the festivals. Franca Bianchini, for her ongoing support of me and this project.
Geri La Duke, for her patience and assistance through the writing of this cookbook. My cousins in Italy,
Gina Buoiano Stefani and Lia Vanucchi Stefani, for sharing so many special dinners together in Lucca.
My cousin Maurice Stefani, for his constant love and support throughout the writing of this book.
All my dear Italian friends in Sacramento who, over the years, tasted my recipes and gave their seal of approval.
And special thanks to Deanna Hanson, for without her inspiration and constant encouragement,
this cookbook probably would not have been written.

CONTENTS

PREFACE

Imagine a special evening with dear friends and family gathered in your home as aromas from a freshly prepared meal mingle and drift through the air. Once the preparations are completed and just before the meal is presented, the sense of excitement increases. Anticipation seizes the hungry as they send up a silent prayer of thanksgiving amid a chorus of "oohs" and "ahhs."

I enjoy the experience of dinner parties so much that I recreate them as often as I can. The meal, after all, is a wonderful celebration—a special occasion that draws loved ones together for an evening of conviviality.

What's more, hosting a dinner party gives me a great reason for cooking Northern Italian cuisine, which has turned out to be an overwhelming favorite among the thousands of dinner guests I have entertained over the years.

My love of cooking can be traced back to my family roots.

My family moved to Sacramento, California, from Lucca, a city located in the Tuscany region of Italy. Although I was born in Sacramento, my home life was predominantly Italian (with immigrant parents, it could hardly have been anything else). Authentic Italian meals were served in the Dinelli home every night. Canned goods and frozen vegetables were never used. Instead, my mother took pride in creating fabulous dishes from scratch, no matter how long it took to prepare them. Mother would often prepare five-course meals for those fun-filled nights when friends came by. Each course, as I remember, seemed better than the one before.

As a small child standing at my mother's side, I began helping in the kitchen, watching at first, handing things to her later, but always learning. After a while, I began cooking most of the meals myself.

Now I find myself cooking for family and friends just as my mother once did.

I frequently return to the Tuscany region to visit family members and to stay in touch with the creativity and authenticity of the region I love so much. During each visit, we work together to recapture the fun and delight of the dinner parties of years past that each family member holds so dear in memory.

The result of these experiences is the cookbook you hold in your hands. Creating this book has been a joyful struggle at times and also a source of great pride. I have carefully selected recipes and offered tips for hosting your own dinner parties with the hope that this cookbook will become a tremendous source of pleasure for you as you share a taste of Lucca with your guests.

Buon appetito!

About This Cookbook

In Italy the dinner is a celebration, a ritual to uphold daily family interaction and social enjoyment. The respect of tradition is illuminated in the "Lucchese kitchen," for it conserves the sweet smells of the past, the wisdom of preparing simple dishes and the true art of cooking.

The recipes in this cookbook represent a collection of dishes I learned from family and friends over the years. Some recipes date back centuries, while others are more recent. All have been prepared with love and affection.

Like all good Italian cooks, I have organized this book into sections reflecting the way Tuscans sit down to eat. True Italian meals start with an antipasto, followed by a *primo,* or first dish of rice, soup or pasta, and a *secondo* of meats accompanied by vegetables, or *contorni.*

No Italian meal would be complete without a colorful spread of fruit and cheese to cleanse the palate. Italy offers a rich variety of cheeses, so I've included a companion guide to cheeses.

Dessert is often the crowning glory of a fine Italian dinner. The Italian poet D'Annunzio said it best: "The real luxury of a meal is in the dessert."

This book opens with a selection of menus and suggestions on how to present an authentic Northern Italian dinner party. Whether for two or 200, Tuscany cuisine and the art of gracious dining are flexible enough to accommodate any event—from a casual get-together to a formal party.

In short, this book is intended to impart a taste of Lucca: the sights, sounds and textures that make this part of Italy such a delight. Read it from cover to cover or browse through the sections at your leisure. Join us as we celebrate the culture and cuisine of Lucca!

HISTORY OF LUCCA

Like an island, Lucca sits in the center of a small but fertile plain, enclosed in walls that are flanked with trees. Within these ancient walls, the towers, churches and palaces still stand, witnesses to Lucca's history and past glory.

In other, neighboring Tuscan towns, the structures are in the Gothic and Renaissance styles. In Lucca, however, many of the buildings are medieval Romanesque, enduring testaments to the Roman era, the period that contributed most to the town's character.

Lucca took on many characteristics of the Roman culture, the most visible being the architecture. The town is adorned with an amphitheater and numerous churches set along its narrow streets. Many homes belonged to powerful and prestigious families and were built with towers. Because the town was located at a major crossroads, it became well known and served as an important military center. This period saw the beginning of the weaving industry—the foundation of Lucca's economic strength for centuries. For example, in Tuscany, the woolen industry became the principal source of commercial and industrial prosperity and Lucca, in particular, was the earliest city to win fame for its silk.

The twelfth and thirteenth centuries witnessed the peak of Lucca's political and economic power, which extended into neighboring Versilia and Garfagnana. The goods that Lucca produced, most importantly its silks, reached all the marketplaces in Europe and the Middle East. During this period, the city renewed itself completely. All the churches were reconstructed and adorned with splendid facades. Many of them, such as San Martino, San Michele and San Frediano, still appear as they did in the thirteenth century.

During this time of rapid growth, Lucca had its share of internal difficulties. Struggles for power arose, first between the political parties of Guelfi and Ghibellini and then between the Bianchi and Neri. In 1400 Paolo Guinigi, a rich and powerful merchant, became the lord of Lucca; he governed the city for approximately 30 years. Evidence of his reign is the famous tree tower, called Torre Guinigi, which still stands inside the walled Lucca.

Reconstructing its independence after the fall of the Guinigi, the republic of Lucca struggled to remain an independent republic during the fifteenth and sixteenth centuries.

Governed by patriarchs, formed exclusively from old, wealthy merchant families, the small republic of Lucca prolonged its aristocracy until 1799, when it fell to Napoleon, who entrusted the town to his sister Elisa, wife of Felice Baciocchi, who belonged to an old noble Lucca family.

After the collapse of the Napoleons, the Congress of Vienna made the city a small duchy under the reign of the Bourbon from Parma family, first under Maria Luisa and then under her son Carlo Ludovico. Architectural changes made during this period can still be seen. It was the ingenious architect Loreno Nottolini who created the stupendous promenade on the walls that enclose Lucca.

After the resignation of Carlo Ludovico, Lucca was united with the grand duchy of Tuscany, and after several years, Lucca became a part of the reigning Italy.

Lucca remains the beautiful walled city in the Tuscany region of Italy.

REMINISCENCES OF LUCCA

When I think of Lucca, images come to mind of autumn with its warm light and fragrant air hanging over the city. It is the time to harvest the olives, chestnuts and grapes. I remember these community events with warm feelings. The work of harvesting would take place in each of the small towns outside the walled city of Lucca. Everyone, young and old, would come together to prepare the future years' supply of wine, olive oil and chestnut flour. After a hard day's work, the women would prepare a dinner to be shared by all amid boasting of whose crop was best that season.

Sundays still bring fond memories. The bells would ring out as we put on our best clothes for church. Afterward, a special meal was prepared with wonderful desserts and special wines. To this day, I can close my eyes and remember walking on Via Fillungo in Lucca, feeling the cobblestones under my feet. I can see the beautiful boutiques and the wonderful cafes filled with people laughing, exchanging conversation and drinking either an aperitif or an espresso.

Early in the morning, I would often hear the toot of a horn, fresh bread being delivered or perhaps the old woman calling out, *"Pesce fresco"* ("Fresh fish"). She pushed an old wooden cart heaped with all types of seafood—squid, mussels, clams, prawns—just about anything you might desire.

There was the fruit and vegetable cart, where a crowd would gather as the vendor weighed purchases of oranges, pears, apples and the like. He wrapped the fresh food in newspapers instead of using bags, and I don't remember ever getting all the eggs home without breaking at least one.

Whenever I visit Lucca, whether in person or in my imagination, I gain a sense of peace. The wonderful green countryside, hills full of olive orchards, chestnut trees and grape vineyards, always brings back warm, vivid memories of this wonderful part of Italy.

Lucca Today

Lucca today is not that much different from the Lucca of centuries past. It is a small town with abundant culture and history. It has many monuments, ancient churches and old streets filled with old-fashioned charm.

The narrow streets, dating from the Middle Ages, lead into cobblestoned squares. The houses are centuries old and boast the beautiful red clay tile roofs that are characteristic of Tuscany. Intent on preserving the past, the province of Lucca protects its heritage from careless renovation, designating the houses as part of the "fine arts."

The ways of Lucca are timeless. The Lucchese, as people of Lucca are called, are still strongly independent and sociable. It is not unusual to see large groups of people strolling through the town on Sundays, enjoying each other's company and calling out to friends and family as they pass.

In the summer, the air around Lucca is especially pungent as the olives are pressed and the tomatoes ripen. A common sight is a wide board set between two chairs and loaded with tomatoes. The tomatoes are first cooked in boiling water then placed in the hot Tuscan sun. As the liquid drips away through the boards, left behind is a thick-cooked paste that the ladies scrape up with spoons and use for making sauces and other tomato-based dishes.

In August, you can see the women of the village striding up the hills. They may be searching for the perfect figs for the day's antipasto or filling their aprons with the herbs used in cooking and folk medicine.

When visiting Lucca, one should try the products typically grown there. Lucca olive oil is world famous for its exquisite taste and unsurpassable quality. The olive oil from this area is delicate but rich in flavor, due greatly to the type of rich and natural soil in which the olive trees grow. Pecorino cheese, which is still made in the traditional ways of local shepherds, is simply delightful. Aged or fresh, pecorino is one of the most flavorful cheeses of the area.

A wide variety of herbs grow wild on the hillsides of Lucca. Many are used for cooking, and some are still used today for medicinal purposes. The wines, the chestnut trees and wild mushrooms all grow in abundance in this rich soil.

FESTIVALS

Food plays an important part in the festivals of Tuscany. Some festivals are dedicated to specific foods, while others, religious in context, feature special dishes served only on the day.

Festivals, called *sagre*, commemorate the traditional dishes of many of the villages around Lucca. Celebrated in the summer and early months of autumn, the *sagre* are lively festivals featuring dancing, local wines and food. Some of the local *sagre* celebrated in Lucca are the *sagre del' olio di oliva* (olive oil), *sagre delle torte* (pies) and *sagre della zuppa di cavolo* (cabbage soup).

Religious festivals punctuate the Tuscan year and provide a reason for families to gather together and enjoy the traditional foods associated with these holidays.

La Vigilia di Natale, Christmas Eve, features a light meal with broth and *baccalà*, dried cod. After midnight mass, Tuscans love to come home to enjoy a large pot of *tullore*, or dried chestnuts boiled in water.

Pasqua, Easter, and *Pasquetta*, Easter Monday, are traditional holidays that feature special breads and meat dishes. In the past, lamb was eaten only for Easter dinner. The *colomba di Pasqua*, a spectacular Easter bread, is still served for both Easter and Easter Monday meals.

Other festivals, or *festas*, include the *Festa di Santa Croce*, a holiday celebrating a holy cross over 1,000 years old, and *Epifania*, Epiphany. During Epiphany, Tuscan households make traditional dunking cookies to offer to the choirs who wander from house to house singing traditional songs.

HOLIDAYS - TRADITIONS

Festa di Santa Croce
Feast of the Holy Cross

For 3 weeks in September, Lucca celebrates this feast. It is the tradition to carry the holy cross from the San Frediano church to the San Martino church. All the communities surrounding Lucca partake in this festive procession. The actual day of *Santa Croce*, and the day of the procession, is September 14. However, there are 3 weeks of celebration, each week after a religious holiday.

The first week celebrates the holy cross; the second week celebrates San Matteo; the third week celebrates San Michele.

This holiday and tradition includes processions, open markets and, of course, plenty of traditional Lucchese foods. The people of Lucca and surrounding communities will wait all year long to buy embroidered towels, table clothes, sweaters, coffee pots, dishes and just about anything you can imagine at the *fiera* (open market). A festive feeling is in the air during these 3 weeks.

Festa della Madonna
Feast of the Virgin Mary

This was an old festival celebrated throughout Italy, falling on September 8. In the old days, the Lucchese would walk miles to the Grotto of the Madonna, located on the hillside of Lucca. They say that, in this grotto, there was a place where drops of water would fall. The tradition was to have one drop of the sacred water fall on your head, which they say would be good for your soul.

Then, of course, the fun begins—walking from Freghino to Quattro Venti, two small towns located on the Lucca hillside. There are picnics, accordion music, folk singing and dancing. The celebration lasts the entire day.

Pasquetta
Little Easter

This holiday name literally translates into "Little Easter." Pasquetta is celebrated on the Monday after Easter as both a national and a traditional holiday. This day is to be spent with family and good friends.

Special picnic baskets are prepared with meats, cheeses, fruits and local wines, followed by a walk up one of the hillsides for a country picnic. This is a simple day to rest, laugh, sing, sleep and simply celebrate the first day after Easter.

La Vigilia di Natale
Christmas Eve

In the old times, it was traditional to eat a light meal with family, usually consisting of a broth, then perhaps some *baccalà*. The local townspeople would go to their respective churches at midnight to celebrate Christmas with a high mass, mostly sung by the local choir, which had been preparing for weeks for this special occasion.

After mass, everyone would return home to enjoy a large pot of *tullore*, dried chestnuts boiled in water, and a glass or two of the local wine. *Tullore* are boiled in water for about 1½ hours, or until they become soft and the water becomes somewhat thick. Eaten in a bowl, *tullore* has the consistency of a thick soup. High in protein, it is a very filling, substantial food.

La Befana
The Good Witch

This is the celebration of Epiphany, which falls on January 6.

La Befana literally translates into "good witch" or "white witch." She represents in Italy what Santa Claus represents in America. She is characterized as an old lady dressed in rags who carries a bag of toys, dried fruits, some candy and small gifts for children.

In the old days, it was traditional for the men's choir of the local villages to sing at the homes of unmarried women. After the choir had finished singing, they would be invited into the house for cookies and wine.

Sagre
Festivals

These festivals commemorate traditional dishes of each village. Groups of local towns-people get together to prepare and cook the most famous traditional dish of their town. Local foods, wines and dancing are part of the *sagre*. Usually a small fee is paid to eat the foods and drink the wines. Extra money is donated to charity.

Some of the local *sagre* celebrated in Lucca are *sagre del' olio di oliva*, *sagre delle torte* and *sagre della zuppa*. These *sagre* are celebrated throughout Italy, usually in the summer and early autumn months.

PLANNING AND HOSTING
A NORTHERN ITALIAN DINNER PARTY

Like my cousins in Lucca, I love to give dinner parties for friends and colleagues. Over the years, I have discovered several ways to keep the process simple while at the same time creating a meal that is pleasing to the taste and to the eye.

The good and gracious outcome of a dinner party depends not only on the ability of the cook, but also on how the dinner is planned. In preparing for a dinner party, the perfect host or hostess should write down everything, from who the dinner guests will be to the entire menu and all ingredients that will be needed.

Tuscan hosts pride themselves not only on their food but on the atmosphere and presentation of the meal. With a little careful planning, you, too, will be able to create a taste of Lucca for your guests.

Inviting Guests

When making a guest list for your dinner party, try to invite people who have something in common so there will be plenty of topics for conversation. Ideally, the total number of people, including yourself, should be no more than eight. More than this, and it can be a difficult to ensure that each guest is taken care of properly.

Two weeks in advance, telephone the guests to invite them for dinner. If they do not give an immediate response, ask them to please RSVP no later than 1 week before the dinner. If you use written invitations, mail them 2 weeks in advance, with an RSVP due 1 week before the dinner. Once you have received all RSVPs and know who will be attending, it's time to start planning the menu.

Planning the Menu

A true Lucchese meal adapts to all seasons and lends itself to casual dining or special celebrations. I love putting a menu together. It is very much like piecing together a puzzle— the antipasto, the first course, the second course, vegetables, dessert and the different wines. I suggest writing out the menu on paper so you can determine more easily if the dishes and wines go well together. You wouldn't serve a meat pasta with an entree of all fish, for example. Sometimes, I'll make copies of the menu for my guests, who seem to enjoy this.

To organize and decide on an ideal menu, consider the likes and dislikes of your guests. When inviting guests with whom I am not familiar, I try not to serve anything too unusual.

When choosing a menu, be aware of what foods a particular season has to offer. For example, fresh tomatoes, fruit and lettuce are best in the summer, while fresh greens, peas and potatoes are excellent in the winter. In general, lighter meals are perfect for the summer, while more substantial dishes are popular winter fare.

Planning the menu also depends greatly on what type of dinner you will be preparing: a light dinner, a hearty country meal, a gourmet dinner or just a fun, casual get-together dinner.

The sequence I follow begins with the antipasto. Then I go to the next courses—*primo*, *secondo* and *dolce*, and I end with the wines. Next to each course I make a list of all ingredients I need to purchase and where I might find them.

Gathering Ingredients

In Italy, giving a dinner party is both an adventure and a celebration. Shopping for vegetables at the *fruttivendolo*—the fruit and vegetable seller—or visiting the fish market early in the morning to get the best of the catch is always an exercise in cheerful bargaining and a bit of a treasure hunt. And you can partake of this adventure, too, no matter where you live!

Once you have settled on your menu, check your supplies. It may be that you have many of the basic ingredients, such as herbs and olive oil, already on hand. If not, put these down on your "to get" list.

Whenever possible, buy fresh herbs. Tuscan cooks like to use nothing but the freshest herbs. Northern Italian cooking is different from its Southern Italian counterpart in that herbs are used sparingly to give the lighter sauces subtle combinations of tastes.

The following herbs are frequently used in Tuscan cooking. Most of these herbs are easily found in local supermarkets. Many Tuscan cooks grow them in gardens:

salvia - sage

rosmarino - rosemary

prezzemolo - Italian parsley

basilico - basil

aglio - garlic

nepitella - mint

timo (pepporino) - thyme

Most of the ingredients can be found easily in local supermarkets. Specialty stores are excellent sources for some ingredients, such as porcini mushrooms and pecorino cheese, that give Lucchese dishes their special taste.

You can organize and purchase the ingredients up to 3 days before the dinner party, depending on what you are serving. Many of the basic items can be shopped for well in advance—such as milk, butter, olive oil and wines. The vegetables can be purchased up to 2 days before your dinner party to ensure freshness. Meats, poultry or fish should be purchased either the day of your dinner party or the day before. Remember that fresh foods are important to the overall flavor of your meal. If you are looking for a special cut, such as a butterflied roast, call ahead and reserve what you need.

No Tuscan dinner party would be complete without a wine list. I always keep chardonnays, cabernets and merlots on hand. I try to serve those wines that best complement the dishes on the menu, ever mindful of my guests' preferences (see wine section, page 191).

Preparing for the Dinner Party

Now that the shopping has been completed and you have the necessary ingredients, you can take several steps the day before so you will have more time to relax as your guests arrive on the day of the dinner party. These include organizing and preparing some of the food. Most lettuces, for example, can be washed and kept in a vegetable bag until ready for use. Then, on the day of your dinner party, you need only place the lettuce in the salad bowl and toss. Vegetables can also be chopped, diced or trimmed and stored. Sometimes, I peel the garlic, wash the herbs and seal them in plastic containers the day before.

These little activities may seem unimportant, but they really cut preparation time.

Soups also can be made the day before. All you would need to do on the evening of the dinner is bring the soup to a boil, add your small pasta or rice and cook. Some sauces for rice can be made the day before your dinner; however, risotti should be made at the last minute to maintain its good texture. Remember, some sauces, such as meat sauce or tomato sauce, can be prepared the day before.

I also will prepare my meat sauce the day before. Some pasta dishes, such as lasagne or cannelloni, can be prepared up to 24 hours in advance and refrigerated. Meats usually can be marinated on the night before or during the early morning on the day of the dinner.

There are many things you can do in advance to ensure that activities during the day of the dinner party go smoothly. I even get out the serving platters that I will be using, as well as any pots or pans I will need the next evening. That way everything is ready to assist me with the dinner.

Setting the Table

Italian tables are a marvel of economy and beauty. A simple tablecloth, attractive plates and silverware and a centerpiece of fresh flowers highlight the food and set guests at ease. I like to use linen tablecloths and set the table in advance, including setting out glasses for the aperitifs.

Your table should be set so that each guest has comfortable sitting and eating space. Typically, I set the table a couple of hours in advance and also do a final check on the wines to make sure the whites are chilled, the reds are uncorked and allowed to breathe, cocktail glasses are set out and ice has been made.

Cooking the Meal

The 2-hour period before your guests arrive is important. By now, everything should have been prepared and can now be cooked easily.

If you have organized correctly, this process should go smoothly. Make sure vegetables have been cut, salads are ready, pots and pans are ready for cooking and condiments and dishes are prepared.

Remember, if you are well organized and plan properly, all will look and feel right. The art of preparing for a dinner party is realizing that it takes preliminary work to make it look easy!

If you are serving a cold antipasto, such as proscuitto and melon, or pinzimonio, it can be prepared at least several hours in advance and refrigerated until ready to serve with the hot antipastos. The bread can be toasted up to 1 hour before, and some of the sauces can be made several hours before and then warmed up. The salad dressing can be made the day before, then refrigerated.

When getting the soups, rices or pasta ready, the trick is to calculate the amount of time you will need to have them completed once the antipasto is served.

Poultry or fish dishes can be marinated during the morning on the day of your dinner party. Some of the meat items need to be prepared that evening and cooked while the antipasto is being served. Roasts are always easy as they can be placed in ovens and require only occasional basting.

Many desserts can be prepared the day before; however, those with creme or fresh fruit should be prepared no earlier than the morning of your dinner party to ensure freshness.

Entertaining Your Guests

The guests are about to arrive. Now is the time to take a deep breath and play some light opera, classical or soft music on the stereo. I find this not only soothing to the cook but also very pleasant for the guests. Music is always played during my dinner parties, from the moment I begin to prepare the meal, to when the guests arrive, until they leave and it's time to clean up. I always try to select music that fits the mood. Opera is almost always at least one selection of my music; it just seems to go hand in hand with Italian food.

When the guests arrive, your meal should be about 1 hour away from being served. I especially enjoy this time because it allows everyone to get comfortable, have an aperitif and mingle while enjoying the music and the appetizing sweet smells from the kitchen. I always make sure my guests have everything they need and they are comfortable. Remember, this is their night out, so you want them to really enjoy themselves. When my guests are busy in conversation, I usually slip away unnoticed and begin to prepare the antipasto dishes and perhaps begin to cook the pasta, depending on how long that particular dish will take. I also slice the bread and place it in a breadbasket on the table.

Serving the Meal

When the guests are ready, I invite them to the table with a call of *"A tavola!"* This is what Tuscans say to call young and old to the table. Dining well has been a Tuscan tradition for centuries. In fact, Tuscans love to boast that in a Tuscan home you will eat better than anywhere else in the world.

I usually begin by pouring the wine, and then I serve the antipasto, either passing it around or offering the platter to each of my guests. As my guests enjoy this part of the meal, I slip away again to set up and serve subsequent courses.

Make sure to allow enough time between courses so that you or your guests are not rushed. This just depends on what you are serving, how the conversation is going and how much time you will need for each particular course preparation. Each course that follows will easily fall into place as long as you have organized and planned well for it. Remember to determine how long each course takes to cook so you'll have an idea of when to begin preparing your antipasto, cooking your pasta or starting your main dish.

When most of the dishes and serving platters are cleared away, I ask if anyone would enjoy fresh fruit with a slice of pecorino or parmigiano. Then I begin to serve the dessert and coffee—usually espresso since it is the only Italian coffee served in Italy. It is usually served in demitasse cups because it is so strong.

Espresso beans are dark-roasted coffee beans. They usually are ground very fine, then packed in an espresso coffee maker. Espresso, macchiato and capuccino are the three typical ways of serving coffee. Espresso and macchiato are usually served after lunch or dinner, and capuccino is served only at breakfast or before noon. Espressos are concentrated and strong; macchiato is espresso with a touch of steamed milk; capuccino is espresso served in a larger cup filled with steamed milk.

After Dinner

Dinner conversation in Italy often continues long after dessert has been eaten. I find that dinner parties in America are no exception. Therefore, I always offer my guests an after-dinner drink, such as brandy, sambuca or anisette in addition to espresso.

After the last guest has gone, I usually relax and recall the evening's fun and laughter and the smiling faces of my friends as they thanked me for an enjoyable evening. It is the look of appreciation in their eyes as they thank me that motivates me to keep developing new recipes and planning my next dinner party. It is truly satisfying. Little wonder, then, that Tuscans say, "When the body is full (from eating), the soul sings."

MENUS

Whether your dinner plans include an intimate dinner for two or a lively evening with a large group of friends, the following menus offer suggestions for an elegant and delicious meal. Keep in mind, however, that these recipes are merely suggestions. Be creative and innovative and do not be afraid to try different ways of cooking Italian. Put some opera on the stereo, have a glass of wine and cook....

•   •

Tutto Pesce (All Fish) Menu

Antipasto
Crostini di pesce
Cannellini con gamberi

Primo
Risotto tutto mare

Secondo
Pesce in forno con patate

Verdure
Insalata mista
Asparagi al limone e prezzemolo

Dolci
Macedonia

•

Pollame (Poultry) Menu

Antipasto
Crostini di olive e funghi
Pinzimonio

Primo
Minestra di verdura passata

Secondo
Pollo arrosto al limone

Verdure
Verdura in forno
Insalata di finochietto

Dolci
Dolce di mele con crema

•

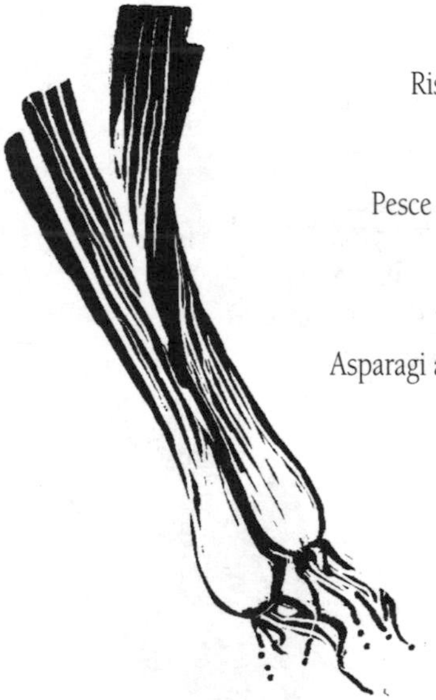

•

Agnello (Lamb) Menu

Antipasto
Crostini di polenta e funghi
Pomodori farciti

Primo
Spaghetti al gorgonzola

Secondo
Spezzatino d'agnello

Verdure
Verdura sfritta
Patate fritte

Dolci
Pesche ripiene

•

•

Manzo (Beef) Menu

Antipasto
Crostini di polenta con salsa rossa
Crostini di fegato

Primo
Pancotto alla Lucchese

Secondo
Saltimbocca Lucchese

Verdure
Fagiolini in umido
Patate al latte

Dolci
Pan di spagna con crema

•

•

Maiale (Pork) Menu

Antipasto
Prosciutto e melone

Primo
Risotto alla parmigiana

Secondo
Spiedini di maiale

Verdure
Fagioli al'ucceletto
Patate arrosto

Dolci
Biscotti

•

•

Tutto Verdura (All Vegetable) Menu

Antipasto
Crostini di olive e funghi
Pinzimonio

Primo
Riso freddo

Secondo
Lasagne ai funghi

Verdure
Carote al marsala
Cavolfiore in bianco
Insalata di finochietto

Dolci
Bigne ripiene

•

•

Fritti (Fried Food) Menu

Primo
Pastina in brodo

Secondo
Fritto misto di pesce

Verdure
Fritto misto di verdure
Insalata mista

Frutta e formaggio
Pera e pecorino

Dolci
Biscotti di mia nonna

•

Invernale (Hearty Winter) Menu

Primo
Farinata

Secondo
Scallopine alla Toscana

Verdure
Fagiolini in umido
Insalata mista

Dolci
Cenci

•

Estivo (Light Summer) Menu

Antipasto
Crostini estivi
Riso freddo

Primo
Linguine al limone

Secondo
Branzino al cartoccio

Verdure
Zucchini e funghi in padella
Insalata di fagioli, cipolla, e pomodoro

Dolci
Crem caramel

•

ANTIPASTI

Literally meaning "before the meal," antipasto is always served before the first course and is always savored in small amounts. It prepares the stomach for the following courses and stimulates the appetite. There are many types of antipasti, which can be as simple as sliced meats and olives or a more elaborate antipasto, such as *polenta crostini con funghi* or *crostini di olive*. Heavier, hot antipasti typically are served with a lighter meal, while lighter, cold antipasti are served with a heartier meal. Sometimes, a variety of antipasto dishes are served followed by only the second dish, leaving out the pasta, rice or soup. The antipasto dish is optional, depending on the complexity or simplicity of the meal. There are many different types of antipasto, typically consisting of *antipasto di mare* (seafood antipasto), *affettati* (sliced cured meats) or *antipasti misti* (mixed antipasti: hot or cold vegetables or meats or both).

An easy summer antipasto.
In Gattaiola, a very small town 2 kilometers from Lucca, there is a special place where you can find a wild fig tree growing. The older ladies of the town will take you there on a very long walk uphill. Once you reach the summit of the hill, you will see a wonderful fig tree with hundreds of white figs. When picking figs, make sure you pick the ones with a drop at the base because these are the sweetest. Bring your treasures home and savor the fruits of your labor with fresh prosciutto.

PROSCIUTTO E MELONE/
PROSCIUTTO E FICHI
Italian Ham with Sliced Melon or Fresh Figs

1	cantaloupe or
12	figs
12	very thin slices of prosciutto

Seed the cantaloupe and slice it into approximately 12 slices, removing the skin. Wrap one slice of prosciutto around each melon slice. Serve cold.

If using fresh figs, wash figs and serve a slice of prosciutto wrapped around each fig.

CROSTINI ALLE OLIVE E FUNGHI
Toasted Bread Squares with Olives and Mushrooms

These crostini are a favorite with many of my guests. Easy to make, this antipasto is deliciously different.

1	10-ounce can black olives, chopped
¼	cup olive oil
½	pound fresh mushrooms
¼	cup Italian parsley, freshly chopped
2	garlic cloves, minced
2	tablespoons dry white wine
8	slices Italian bread
	salt and pepper

In a small bowl, combine the chopped olives and 2 tablespoons of olive oil. Mix well.

Wash, dry and coarsely chop the mushrooms. In a small pan, add 2 tablespoons of the olive oil, chopped mushrooms, fresh parsley, minced garlic, salt and pepper. Gently sauté over low heat for 5 minutes. Add the wine and continue to cook over low heat for an additional 10 minutes.

Toast the bread and cut it into 3-inch squares. Place a small amount of the olive mixture on each slice. Then add a tablespoon of mushrooms on top. Best if served warm.

MEDIUM

Mangia, bevi, e tira a campa'!
(Eat, drink and be merry!)

CROSTINI DI POLENTA ALLA SALSA DI FUNGHI
Roasted Polenta Squares with Zesty Mushroom Sauce

polenta (see p. 49 for recipe)
- ¼ cup olive oil
- 1 celery stalk, finely chopped
- ½ medium yellow onion, finely chopped
- ½ pound fresh mushrooms, finely chopped
- ½ teaspoon red hot chili pepper, finely chopped
- 2 garlic cloves, minced
- ¼ cup Italian parsley, freshly chopped
- 1 8-ounce can tomato sauce
- 3 tablespoons white wine
- 1 tablespoon salt

Cool the polenta for 15 minutes Then pour it into a large rectangular pan about 2 inches deep. Allow to cool for approximately 1 hour. When the polenta is firm, cut it into 2-inch squares.

Preheat oven to 375 degrees. Place the polenta squares on a cookie sheet and roast on each side for about 15 minutes.

ZESTY MUSHROOM SAUCE

Heat the olive oil in a sauce pan. Add the chopped onion and celery and cook on medium heat for approximately 5 minutes. Add the chopped mushrooms and cook over low heat for 10 more minutes. Add the chopped chili pepper flakes, garlic, salt and chopped parsley and mix well. Add the tomato sauce and wine. Allow the mushrooms to cook for about 20 minutes over low heat.

When the sauce is ready, place 1 tablespoon of mushroom sauce on each piece of roasted polenta and serve immediately.

MEDIUM

CROSTINI ALLE VONGOLE
Toasted Bread Squares with Clam Sauce

¼ cup olive oil
½ cup Italian parsley, freshly chopped
3 garlic cloves, minced
1 12-ounce can clams
½ teaspoon red hot chili pepper, finely chopped
½ cup dry white wine
1 teaspoon salt
8 slices Italian bread

In a medium saucepan, heat the olive oil, add the chopped garlic and the chopped parsley and sauté over low heat for 5 minutes.

Add the clams, salt and chili pepper and mix well. Add the wine and continue to cook for 10 minutes on low heat.

Toast 8 slices of Italian bread and cut them into quarters. Place approximately 1 tablespoon of the clam sauce on each quarter of toasted bread and serve immediately.

In Viareggio, a small town on the coast near Lucca, the most fun is finding the small clams on the beach and bringing them home to cook. When I say fresh, I mean fresh!

I love to serve pinzimonio in the summertime, when the onions and tomatoes are in season. This is a great starter when barbecuing.

PINZIMONIO
Mixed Raw Vegetables with Oil and Vinegar Dressing

6	green onions
1	fennel bulb
2	carrots
2	celery stalks
1	tomato
½	cup olive oil
2	tablespoons red wine vinegar
1	teaspoon salt
1	teaspoon pepper
1	garlic clove, minced

Wash, slice, sliver and arrange vegetables on a vegetable tray.

Combine the olive oil, vinegar, salt, pepper and minced garlic clove. Whisk well. Place in a small bowl in the middle of the vegetable tray.

Dip the vegetables in the mixture.

EASY

CROSTINI DI FEGATO
Toasted Bread Squares with Liver Paté

3 tablespoons olive oil
2 garlic cloves, minced
½ medium onion, finely chopped
¾ cup chicken livers
4 sage leaves, freshly chopped
1 tablespoon lemon juice
8 slices Italian bread
   salt and pepper

Heat the olive oil in a saucepan, add the chopped garlic and onion and sauté over low heat for about 5 minutes. Add the chicken livers, sage, salt and pepper and continue to cook for 5 more minutes.

Remove the chicken livers and place them in a food processor. Also add the sauce in which the liver was cooked and the lemon juice. Liver paté should have a smooth consistency. Return the mixture to the saucepan and continue to cook for approximately 3 minutes over low heat.

Toast the bread and cut it into 3-inch squares. Place a teaspoon of liver sauce on each piece. These should be served hot.

Chicken liver crostini are a classic component of Lucchese antipasto. A slice of black olive or a pinch of fresh parsley can be used to top each bread square.

This type of crostini is always best when prepared with fresh tomatoes.

Quando il corpo è pieno, l'anima canta.
(When the stomach is full, the soul sings.)

CROSTINI ESTIVI
Toasted Bread Squares with Fresh Tomatoes and Herbs

3   medium-firm tomatoes, chopped,
    seeds removed
½   medium red onion, finely chopped
¼   cup basil, freshly chopped
¼   cup Italian parsley, freshly chopped
⅓   cup olive oil
3   tablespoons wine vinegar
1   tablespoon capers
8   slices Italian bread
    salt and pepper

In a small bowl, combine the tomatoes, red onion, basil and parsley. Add the olive oil, vinegar, capers, salt and pepper and mix well.

Toast the bread and cut it into 4-inch squares. Place one heaping tablespoon of the mixture on each square and serve.

CANNELLINI CON GAMBERETTI
Cannellini Beans with Prawns

⅔   cup olive oil
1   pound medium prawns
3   garlic cloves, minced
½   cup Italian parsley, freshly chopped
2   tablespoons white wine
2   celery stalks, finely chopped
3   15-ounce cans cannellini beans
    salt

Clean and devein the prawns. In a small skillet, add 1 tablespoon of the olive oil. When the oil is heated, add the prawns. Add 1 minced garlic clove and 1 tablespoon of chopped parsley to the prawns. Next, add the wine and sauté gently for 3 to 4 minutes over medium heat. When cooked, remove the prawns from the juice and place them in a bowl to cool.

Rinse the cannellini beans well with cold water and drain thoroughly. Pour them into a larger serving dish and mix in the remainder of the garlic, celery, parsley, salt, pepper and olive oil.

Add all but 6 prawns to the beans and mix well. Place the remaining prawns on top of the beans and add sprigs of fresh parsley to garnish.

This antipasto dish turned out to be a favorite of many of my guests, as well as a personal favorite of mine. If any is left over, save it for the next day, when the flavors really take hold.

RISO FREDDO
Cold Vegetable Rice

This dish can be prepared a day ahead. It also can be refrigerated for up to a week.

2   cups arborio rice
1   8-ounce can marinated artichokes
1   8-ounce can marinated mushrooms
1   16-ounce jar giardiniera
    (pickled Italian vegetables)
1   6-ounce can pimento olives
1   small red onion, finely chopped
2   celery stalks, chopped
1   4-ounce can black olives, chopped
½   cup olive oil
3   tablespoons lemon juice
    salt

Cook the arborio rice in about 6 cups of salted water for approximately 15 minutes. When the rice is cooked, drain well and place it in a large bowl.

Coarsely chop the artichokes, mushrooms, olives, onion, celery and pickled vegetables and combine them with the rice. Add the olive oil, lemon juice and salt. Combine well.

Allow to refrigerate for 1 hour before serving.

VARIATION
Add tuna, chopped hard-boiled eggs or diced ham

Crostini di Polenta con Salsa al Peperone Rosso
Polenta Squares with Red Bell Pepper Sauce

    polenta (see page 49 for recipe)
½   teaspoon salt
2   red bell peppers
¼   cup olive oil
½   red onion, chopped
2   tablespoons tomato sauce
¼   cup white wine

Wash and seed the bell peppers. Heat ¼ cup of the olive oil. Slice the onion and add it to the heated olive oil. Thinly slice the bell peppers and add them to the olive oil. Then add the salt, tomato sauce and wine. Allow to cook over low heat for 20 minutes. Place the bell peppers and sauce in a food processor and puree until smooth. Return the sauce to the pot and continue to cook for 5 more minutes over low heat.

Cool the polenta for 15 minutes. Then pour it into a large rectangular pan about 2 inches deep. Allow to cool for approximately 1 hour. When the polenta is firm, cut it into 2-inch squares.

Preheat oven to 375 degrees. Place the polenta squares on a cookie sheet and roast on each side for about 15 minutes.

When the polenta is ready, place the squares on a platter and spread them with 1 tablespoon of the bell pepper mixture. Serve hot.

MEDIUM

This antipasto dish is very colorful and very tasty. Polenta can be prepared a day before and placed on a large platter, cut and then refrigerated until you are ready to grill.

PRIMI

SOUPS
RICE
PASTA

Literally meaning "the first" course, il primo generally is served after the antipasto and before the main entree. It usually consists of a soup, rice or pasta dish. These first courses are seldom the main course in Italy, where soup, rice or pasta usually is served only in small amounts—just enough to stimulate the appetite and leave the desire for more. The soups can be rustic or elegant, but they are always tasty and satisfying. Some soups are made with vegetables; others are basic broths with pastina. Some soups are thick and substantial, while others are simple and light. Rice can be used in soups; however, the more popular and classic version is in risotto. Risotto can be made with a variety of sauces from fish, meats or vegetables. Northern Italians use arborio rice, a shorter, plump rice. Risotto has a creamy but not mushy texture. Pasta is by far the single most important food in Italy. Pasta is economical and healthy and it also nourishes, sustains and satisfies. It can be a simple everyday food or an elegant dish. Pasta is a main staple in Italy and can be made in a variety of ways—baked, stuffed or boiled—accompanied with a variety of sauces.

In Italy, the brodo, or broth, is made about twice a week. It is served with pastina and eaten as a first course. Grated Parmesan cheese is sometimes added to a bowl of broth. The boiled chicken typically is eaten as the second course.

"*La gallina vecchia fa buon brodo.*"
An old stewing hen makes good broth.

VARIATION

Ideally, the best meat for making broth would be a stewing hen, which gives your broth an incredibly good flavor.

BRODO
Basic Chicken Broth

1   3-pound chicken, cut into quarters
6   quarts cold water
2   celery stalks with leaves
2   carrots
1   medium yellow onion
1   Italian parsley sprig
2   medium tomatoes
    salt

Wash and dry the chicken. Put all the ingredients into a stock pot with water and place on high heat until the water comes to a full boil. Allow to cook on low heat for approximately 1½ hours, occasionally skimming the top of the broth to remove any fat. When the broth is cooked, pour it through a strainer so that the broth remains clear.

EASY

MINESTRA DI CECI
Garbanzo Bean Soup

¼ cup olive oil
3 garlic cloves, peeled
4 tablespoons tomato sauce
3 fresh rosemary sprigs
2 cups dried garbanzo beans* or
   2 sixteen-ounce cans of garbanzo beans
3 cups chicken broth
   salt and pepper

In a saucepan, add the olive oil, garlic cloves, tomato sauce and rosemary sprigs. Cook over low heat for approximately 10 minutes. Remove the rosemary sprigs and set sauce aside.

If using canned beans, cook them in 4 quarts of water. Bring them to a full boil. Then continue to cook them on medium heat for about 20 minutes.

Place the garbanzo beans, 3 cups of the water in which the garbanzo beans were cooked and the sauce into a blender or food processor and puree. Put the soup back into the pot, add 3 cups of chicken broth, bring to a full boil and add 8 ounces of small pasta (e.g., small shells, elbow macaroni). Continue to cook until the pasta is *al dente*.

Serve with a garnish of fresh rosemary sprig on each bowl of soup.

If using dried garbanzo beans, soak them in cold water overnight. Then cook them for 45 minutes over low heat in plenty of water.

 MEDIUM

A typical Lucchese soup, it is often prepared on Christmas Eve along with baccalà (dried cod) and cooked garbanzo beans. At one time, minestra di ceci was considered a peasant's meal.

MINESTRONE
Vegetable Soup

1 16-ounce bag dried beans (pinto, cranberry or cannellini beans)
½ cup olive oil
½ cup tomato sauce
4 medium potatoes
5 carrots
2 celery stalks

1 small cabbage
3 zucchini
1 10-ounce pack of frozen peas or 1 cup fresh peas
1 cup of fresh Swiss chard, chopped
6 cups chicken broth
salt and pepper

SOUP BASE

½ cup yellow onion, chopped
1 carrot, finely chopped
1 celery stalk, finely chopped
3 garlic cloves, minced

These vegetables are used as sfritto, a base for your soup.

VARIATION

Add small pasta shells or rice to soup. Cook to desired tenderness. The more vegetables you add to minestrone, the more flavorful and colorful it is.

Allow the dried beans to soak in water for approximately 12 hours. Cook the beans in 12 cups of water with a pinch of salt and one of the garlic cloves until beans are tender. Beans should be cooked slowly over low heat.

In a medium-sized saucepan, sauté the chopped onion, chopped carrot, chopped celery, 2 minced garlic cloves in olive oil for about 5 minutes on low heat. Add the tomato sauce and continue to sauté for another 5 minutes. This is the soup base.

Place half of the cooked beans in a blender with about 1 cup of the liquid in which the beans were cooked, add the sautéed vegetables and puree until smooth.

Dice and cut all the vegetables, place in a stock pot, add 6 cups of the chicken broth and 6 cups of water and allow the soup to come to a full boil. Add the pureed vegetables, salt and pepper and cook over low heat for 45 minutes.

 MEDIUM

PANCOTTO ALLA LUCCHESE
Lucca-Style Cooked Bread Soup

3 garlic cloves, minced
¼ medium onion
¼ cup Italian parsley, chopped
½ cup olive oil
1 cup fresh tomatoes, chopped
6 cups day-old sourdough bread, chopped
4 cups chicken broth
1 cup water
  Parmesan cheese (optional)
  salt and pepper

Finely chop the garlic, onion and parsley.

In a medium pot, add the olive oil and chopped onion, garlic and parsley. Allow to sauté for about 10 minutes on low heat. Add the tomatoes and continue to cook on low heat for approximately 10 minutes.

Cut the bread into small pieces (about 1 to 2 inches wide), add the bread to the pot, mix well and then add 4 cups of the broth and 1 cup of water. Salt and pepper to taste and cook over low heat for 15 minutes.

Serve in a soup bowl and sprinkle with Parmesan cheese if desired.

Pancotto is a thick, traditional soup from the countryside surrounding Lucca. In the old days, it was eaten frequently simply because it is a delicious, inexpensive soup that is very filling.

Il pancotto non fa mai vergogna.
(Never be ashamed to serve a simple soup.)

Farinata is a traditional dish specific to the city of Lucca. A hearty dish, it is great for a cold winter night, but it requires the patience, love and luxury of time that cooks once had to spend in the kitchen preparing hearty, simple meals. If you have the time and patience, give it a try. I'm sure you'll enjoy it.

Tanti cuochi fan la minestra sciocca
(Too many cooks spoil the broth)

FARINATA
Minestrone with Corn Meal

1½ cups polenta
2 cups dark green curly cabbage
  minestrone (see page 34 for recipe)
  virgin olive oil

Prepare the minestrone. (The only other item that should be added to the minestrone for this particular dish is 2 cups of dark green curly cabbage. This should be added when the other vegetables are added to the soup.)

Bring the cooked minestrone soup to a boil, slowly stirring in the cornmeal a small amount at a time. Continue to stir until all the cornmeal has been added. Stir the soup frequently so lumps do not form. Allow to simmer over low heat for approximately 45 minutes, stirring continuously.

Serve the farinata in individual bowls. Pour a small amount of virgin olive oil on top of each bowl.

 MEDIUM

MINESTRA DI FAGIOLI
Bean Soup

1 pound dried cannellini beans
   or dried cranberry beans
4 garlic cloves
3 fresh sage sprigs
½ yellow onion, chopped
1 carrot, chopped
1 celery stalk, chopped
½ cup olive oil
½ cup tomato sauce
4 cups water from cooked beans
6 cups chicken broth or water
   salt and pepper

This soup dish is also very typical of the Lucca area. A hearty soup, it can be made with fresh or dried beans.

Soak the dried beans overnight in water.

In a soup pot, bring 6 quarts of water to a boil and add the beans, 2 garlic cloves and fresh sage and cook over low heat for approximately 1 hour or until the beans are tender.

Finely chop the onion, carrot, celery and the remaining garlic cloves. In a pan, add the olive oil and sauté the chopped vegetables over low heat for about 10 minutes, add the tomato sauce and continue to cook for approximately 10 more minutes.

In a food processor or a blender, add 2 cups of the water in which the beans were cooked, about ½ of the beans and ½ of the sautéed vegetables and blend until smooth. Place in a large bowl. Add the remaining beans and sautéed vegetables to the blender and blend until smooth. Return all the blended beans to the pot, and add the chicken broth.

Continue to cook over low heat for 20 minutes, bringing the soup to a boil, and add 1 cup of small pasta shells or ½ cup of rice. Cook the pasta shells for 12 minutes, the rice for 15 minutes.

 MEDIUM

MINESTRA DI VERDURA PASSATA
Pureed Vegetable Soup

This soup is excellent with toasted Italian bread squares. Toast sliced Italian bread, cut it into 1-inch squares, rub them with garlic and float them on top of the soup.

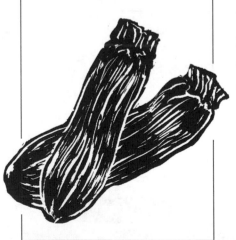

12	ounces cannellini beans (dried or canned)
½	cup olive oil
½	medium yellow onion
1	garlic clove, minced
½	cup tomato sauce
1	fresh parsley sprig
2	carrots
1	celery stalk
4	medium potatoes
2	medium zucchini
¼	pound fresh peas or 1 box frozen peas
6	cups chicken broth
3	cups water in which the beans were cooked
	salt and pepper

If using dried beans, soak them for at least 12 hours. Bring 10 cups of salted water to a boil, and cook beans for 1 hour over low heat.

In a stock pot, heat the olive oil and add the chopped onion. Sauté for approximately 5 minutes over medium heat. Reduce heat, add the chopped garlic and sauté for another 2 minutes. Then add the tomato sauce and sprig of parsley and continue to sauté for approximately 10 minutes. Add the chopped vegetables to the stock pot and mix well. Add the beans, salt, pepper, 6 cups of the chicken broth and 3 cups of the water in which the beans were cooked and continue cooking over low heat for 45 minutes.

In a food processor or blender, add the vegetable soup and puree until smooth. Return the pureed soup to the pot, bring to a boil and serve.

MEDIUM

MINESTRA DI FARRO
Spelt Soup

12	ounces dried cannellini or dried cranberry beans
9	ounces spelt
1	medium onion, chopped
2	celery stalks, chopped
1	carrot, chopped
½	cup olive oil
1	fresh sage sprig
2	cups chicken broth
¼	cup extra virgin olive oil
	salt
⅓	cup olive oil

Soak the spelt overnight in cold water. Put all the ingredients into a large pot. Pour in the broth and enough water to cover the ingredients. Bring to a boil and then simmer over low heat with the cover on for approximately 2 hours. When serving farro, drizzle each soup bowl with a tablespoon of extra virgin olive oil.

Minestra di farro is a hearty soup typical of the area around Lucca because farro grows in abundance in Garfagnana, the fields and countryside just outside Lucca.

VARIATION

Spelt can be found in natural food stores. As a last resort, use pearl barley.

This is a very popular way of serving rice. There are many different ways to combine vegetables, meat or fish when it accompanies rice.

Chi vuol vivere e star bene prenda il mondo come viene.
(If you wish to live happily, take life as it comes.)

RISOTTO AI CARCIOFI
Rice with Artichokes

1	pound small artichokes*
½	lemon
¼	cup olive oil
1	small yellow onion, chopped
2	garlic cloves, minced
½	teaspoon fresh mint, chopped
1	cup arborio rice
2	cups chicken broth
¼	cup dry white wine
½	cup Parmesan cheese, freshly grated
1	teaspoon salt

Remove all the tough outer leaves from the artichokes, cut off the hard tips and wash the artichokes well. Slice the artichokes thinly and place the slices in a bowl of cold water with the lemon. In a medium-sized pot, heat the olive oil and add the chopped onion. Allow to sauté for 10 minutes or until golden brown. Dry the artichoke slices, add them to the pot and mix well. Add the minced garlic and mint, and sauté over low heat for about 15 minutes or until the artichokes are tender. Then add rice, mix well and add 2 cups of the chicken broth, salt and wine, cover and simmer over low heat for 20 minutes, stirring only once while it cooks. When the rice is cooked, mix in the Parmesan cheese. Garnish with fresh mint leaves.

Small artichokes are usually found only in specialty stores. If these are unavailable, frozen artichokes may be used. Marinated or regular large artichokes should not be substituted.

EASY

RISOTTO ALLA PARMIGIANA
Creamy Rice with
Fresh Parmesan Cheese

3	tablespoons olive oil
4	tablespoons butter
2	tablespoons onion, chopped
1	cup arborio rice
1	teaspoon salt
3	cups chicken broth
1½	cups Parmesan cheese, freshly grated

In a medium pot, heat the oil and butter and add the chopped onion. Sauté over low heat for 10 minutes. Add the rice and salt and combine well. Gradually add ½ of the chicken broth and stir, add ⅓ of the cheese and continue to stir over low heat.

When most of the liquid has evaporated, add the remainder of the broth, mix in the remainder of the cheese and continue to stir over low heat until the rice is cooked. Add more broth if needed to cook the rice completely (approximately 20 minutes). Risotto should have a creamy texture. Serve immediately.

This is a creamy rice dish with a consistency similar to that of a thick soup.

RISO AI FUNGHI PORCINI
Rice with Porcini Mushrooms

⅓ cup dried porcini mushrooms
(found in specialty stores)
½ cup water in which the mushrooms
were soaked
½ medium yellow onion, finely chopped
¼ cup olive oil
1 cup arborio rice
salt and pepper
3 cups chicken broth
½ cup Parmesan cheese, grated

Soak the dried porcini mushrooms in hot water for about 10 minutes. Then remove them from the water (retain the water in which the mushrooms were soaked). Finely chop the onion and porcini mushrooms separately. In a medium pot, heat the olive oil and add the onions. Allow to sauté over low heat for approximately 5 minutes. Add the porcini mushrooms and continue to sauté over low heat for 10 minutes. Add the rice, salt and pepper and combine well. Next, add the broth and ½ cup of the water in which the dried porcini were soaked and cook covered for 18 minutes on low heat. When the rice is cooked, add the Parmesan cheese, mix well and serve immediately.

EASY

RISOTTO SAPORITO
Savory Rice

Arborio rice, a plump, oval-shaped rice, is at its finest when cooked in risotto.

  1 small red onion, finely chopped
  1 celery stalk, finely chopped
  1 carrot, finely chopped
  ⅓ cup olive oil
  3 medium tomatoes
  ¼ cup Italian parsley, chopped
  2 tablespoons basil, freshly chopped
  2 garlic cloves, minced
  1 teaspoon salt
  ½ teaspoon red hot chili pepper, finely chopped
1¼ cup arborio rice
  2 cups chicken broth
  ½ cup pecorino cheese, grated

Finely chop the onion, celery and carrot. In a medium pot, heat the olive oil and add the chopped vegetables. Slowly cook over low heat for approximately 10 minutes.

Skin and seed the tomatoes, chop them finely and add them to the sautéed vegetables. Add the chopped parsley, basil, garlic, salt and pepper. Continue to cook over low heat for 25 minutes. When the sauce has finished cooking, add the rice, mix well and add the chicken broth. Bring to a full boil. Then cook the rice covered for approximately 16 minutes over low heat. When the rice is cooked, sprinkle with the fresh pecorino cheese and serve immediately.

Garnish with fresh basil and parsley sprigs.

EASY

RISOTTO TUTTO PESCE
Rice with Fish

½	pound medium prawns	3	tablespoons Italian parsley, chopped
¼	pound small squid	½	cup white wine
8	fresh clams	½	cup ripe tomatoes, chopped
8	fresh mussels	¼	lemon
½	pound halibut or other firm white fish	1½	cups arborio rice
⅓	cup olive oil	2	teaspoons salt
2	garlic cloves, minced	1½	cups fish stock
¼	teaspoon red hot chili pepper, finely chopped	1	cup water

Peel, devein and wash the prawns. Cut ½ of the prawns into 1-inch pieces, leaving the remainder whole. Wash the squid, removing the ink sac, and cut it into 1-inch pieces. Steam the clams and mussels, discard those that have not opened and retain a ½ cup of the liquid.

In a medium pot, heat the oil. Add the minced garlic and chopped chili peppers and sauté over low heat for 3 minutes. Add the parsley and all the fish and cook for approximately 5 minutes, Then add the white wine. When the wine has almost evaporated, add the tomatoes and lemon and continue to cook for approximately 10 minutes. Add the rice and salt and mix well with the fish sauce. Gradually add the fish stock and water until the rice is cooked, stirring occasionally.

This rice is a classic dish served in Viareggio. The more varieties of fish, the tastier the risotto.

When the rice is cooked, transfer it to a serving platter, sprinkle it with parsley and garnish with fresh mussels and clams.

 MEDIUM

RISO IN BIANCO
White Rice with Butter and Onion

1   small yellow onion, chopped
6   tablespoons butter
1   cup arborio rice
2   cups chicken broth
    salt

Finely chop the onion. In a medium pot, melt the butter over low heat. Add the onion and continue to cook for 7 minutes over low heat. Add the rice and salt and stir well. Add the hot chicken broth and bring to a boil. Lower heat, cover the rice and continue to cook over low heat for 18 minutes.

This is a simple rice dish that can be served as an accompaniment to almost any poultry, lamb or meat dish.

RISOTTO ALLA POMAROLA
Rice with Fresh Tomato and Herbs

4	medium tomatoes
1	carrot, chopped
½	medium onion (yellow or red)
1	celery stalk, chopped
¼	cup olive oil
2	garlic cloves, minced
¼	cup parsley, freshly chopped
2	tablespoons basil, freshly chopped
	salt and pepper
1½	cups arborio rice
¼	cup Parmesan cheese, freshly grated
2½	cups water
½	cup chicken broth

In a medium pot, bring the water to a boil. Add the tomatoes for
2 minutes and remove. Peel the skin from the tomatoes, squeeze
them to remove the excess seeds and chop them coarsely.

Finely chop the carrot, chop the onion and dice the celery. In a
medium pot, add the olive oil and heat. Add the celery, carrot and
onion and simmer over low heat for 10 minutes. Add the
chopped tomatoes, garlic, parsley and basil. Continue to cook
over low heat for 10 minutes. Add the salt and pepper and cook
on low heat for approximately 15 minutes. Place the sauce in a
food processor or blender and puree. Return the sauce to the pot,
add the rice to the tomato sauce and mix well. Add water and
broth and allow the mixture to come to a full boil. Cover and
cook over low heat for 20 minutes.

Add the Parmesan cheese and sprinkle with
chopped fresh parsley.

EASY

RISOTTO CON SUGO DI CARNE
Rice with Meat Sauce

1½   cups meat sauce (see page 152 for recipe)
1¼   cups arborio rice
2½   cups chicken broth
  ½   cup Parmesan cheese, freshly grated
     salt

Prepare the meat sauce. When the sauce is cooked, add the rice and mix well. Add the broth to the rice and bring the mixture to a boil. Reduce the heat, add the salt, cover and cook over low heat for 18 minutes.

When the rice is cooked, sprinkle with the grated Parmesan cheese.

MEDIUM

Rice is a popular staple on Tuscan tables. The creative Tuscan cook dresses it up with a meat, vegetable or fish sauce.

This rice dish is best when the asparagus is fresh. I often steam an extra 8 to 10 spears and garnish the rice with them.

RISO CON ASPARAGI
Rice with Asparagus

1½ pounds fresh asparagus
½ medium onion, chopped
¼ cup olive oil
1 tablespoon butter
½ cup dry white wine
1¼ cups arborio rice
2 cups chicken broth
½ cup water
3 tablespoons Parmesan cheese, grated
   salt

Wash, trim and discard the tougher part of the asparagus stalks. Dice the asparagus and finely chop the onion.

In a medium pot, heat the olive oil and butter. Add the onion and sauté over low heat for 5 minutes. Add the diced asparagus and continue to cook over low heat for 5 minutes. Add the white wine and cook until the wine has evaporated and the asparagus is tender.

Add the rice and mix well. Turn heat to high and add 2 cups of the broth and ½ cup of water. When the rice mixture comes to a full boil, add the salt and lower the heat. Cover and continue to cook for 15 minutes.

When the rice is cooked, add the grated cheese and serve.

POLENTA
Cornmeal

- 8 cups water
- 1 teaspoon salt
- 1 teaspoon olive oil
- 3 cups polenta

Bring water to a boil in a large pot. Add the salt and olive oil.
Reduce heat and gradually add small amounts of the polenta,
stirring constantly with a wooden spoon. Continue to add the
polenta and stir until all of it has been added to the water. Stir
vigorously to avoid lumps. The polenta will gradually thicken as it
cooks. Cook and stir for about 45 minutes. The polenta is cooked
when it clearly comes away from the sides of the pot.

Polenta can be served many
ways, with a chicken tomato
sauce, butter and cheese or even
a mushroom sauce.

*Chi ha fame, mangia anche
la polenta fredda.*
(If one is hungry, even a slice of
cold polenta will do.)

This spaghetti dish is served in almost every restaurant in Viareggio. Excellent in flavor and easy to make.

SPAGHETTI ALLE VONGOLE
Spaghetti with Clams

1	pound fresh clams
½	cup parsley, freshly chopped
4	garlic cloves, minced
⅓	cup olive oil
1	15-ounce can small clams
½	cup white wine
¼	teaspoon red hot chili pepper, chopped
1	pound spaghetti
	salt

Place the clams in a large bowl, scrub well with cold water and rinse. After cleaning the clams, place them in a large pot with a ½ cup of water. Bring to a boil and allow to steam for about 5 minutes or until all the clams have opened. Discard clams that have not opened.

Finely chop the parsley and mince the garlic. Heat the olive oil in a medium-sized pot. Then place the cleaned fresh clams, along with their shells and the canned clams, in the pot. Allow to gently simmer on low heat for approximately 2 minutes. Add the chopped parsley and garlic, stirring so that all the clams are well mixed with the parsley and garlic. Add the white wine, chili pepper and salt and allow them to simmer on low heat for 10 minutes.

Cook the spaghetti until *al dente*. When the pasta is cooked, drain well and place the cooked spaghetti in a sauce pan with the clam sauce. Mix well and continue to cook on low heat for 3 minutes, mixing the pasta with the sauce.

 MEDIUM

VARIATION
Mussels also can be added to this pasta dish when the clam shells are added.

SPAGHETTI CON AGLIO, OLIO E PEPERONCINO
Spaghetti with Garlic, Olive Oil and Chili Pepper

1	pound spaghetti
4	garlic cloves, minced
2	fresh basil leaves
½	cup olive oil
1	teaspoon red hot chili pepper, finely chopped
	salt

Cook the spaghetti in a large pot of salted water.

Mince the garlic and finely chop the chili pepper. Coarsely chop the basil.

In a small saucepan, heat the olive oil over low heat. Add the garlic and chopped chili pepper and continue to cook for 3 minutes over low heat. Do not allow the garlic to burn or turn brown. Take the sauce off the burner and add the basil leaves.

When the spaghetti is cooked, drain well and combine the sauce with the pasta. Serve immediately.

EASY

This is a favorite midnight snack in Italy. A light and tasty pasta, it leaves you with the desire for more. On my most recent trip to Italy, I visited with a friend and we talked until the wee hours of the morning. At about 1:00 a.m., we decided we were hungry, so we made *spaghetti con aglio e olio* and opened up a bottle of champagne. I don't remember all of the conversation we had that night, but I distinctly remember how good the pasta tasted with champagne.

I often prepare pesto and freeze it during the summer, when there is an abundance of fresh basil. I leave out the pine nuts, adding them when pasta is made.

TRENETTE AL PESTO
Trenette with Pesto

3	garlic cloves, minced
¼	cup Italian parsley, freshly chopped
½	cup basil, freshly chopped
⅓	cup olive oil
¼	cup toasted pine nuts (optional)
1	teaspoon salt
¼	cup Parmesan cheese, freshly grated
1	pound trenette

I make pesto sauce two ways, both of which are described below.

The following recipe has parsley but no pine nuts:

Finely chop the garlic, parsley and basil. (A food processor can be used instead of doing the chopping by hand.) Bring a large pot of salted water to a boil, add the pasta and cook until *al dente*.

Combine the olive oil, chopped parsley, basil, garlic and salt.

When the pasta is cooked, drain well and combine with the pesto sauce. Add the cheese and toss the pasta.

The following recipe has toasted pine nuts but no parsley and is a smoother sauce:

Combine the basil, garlic and salt in a food processor and slowly add the olive oil until a smooth consistency has been achieved. Place in a bowl and add toasted pine nuts and cheese.

Cook the pasta, drain well and mix with sauce.

Farfalle al Salmone
Butterfly Noodles with Salmon Sauce

½ cup olive oil
¾ pound fresh salmon fillet (skin removed)
1 teaspoon rosemary, freshly chopped
2 garlic cloves, minced
½ cup Italian parsley, freshly chopped
1 teaspoon lemon rind, grated
 salt and pepper
½ cup dry white wine
¼ teaspoon red hot chili pepper,
 finely chopped
1 pound farfalle

Pour 1 teaspoon of olive oil onto the fillet and sprinkle with ½ teaspoon of chopped rosemary. Lay the fillet on a broiler pan and broil it for approximately 8 minutes.

Mince the garlic and finely chop the remaining parsley. Preheat the olive oil in a medium sauce pan. Add the chopped parsley, garlic and lemon rind and sauté on low heat for approximately 3 minutes. When the salmon is cooked, gently cut it into large chunks and add it to the olive oil. Add the salt, pepper and ¼ cup of the wine and continue to cook for 5 minutes. Add the chopped chili pepper and the remainder of the wine. Continue to cook over low heat for 8 minutes.

In a large pot, bring salted water to a boil and add the butterfly noodles. Cook as directed. Drain well and then toss well with the sauce and serve immediately.

Sprinkle with freshly chopped parsley.

This pasta dish is almost a meal in itself. I enjoy this salmon pasta with a mixed green salad and, of course, a chilled glass of chardonnay.

 MEDIUM

LINGUINE VIAREGGINE
Viareggio-Style Linguine

1 pound clams	1 teaspoon red hot chili pepper, finely chopped
½ cup olive oil	
2 garlic cloves, minced	½ cup white wine
¾ pound medium prawns	12 ounces fresh tomatoes (canned Italian plum tomatoes are also very good)
½ pound calamari	
12 ounces halibut fillet	
1 small onion, chopped	1 pound linguine
3 tablespoons parsley, freshly chopped	

Soak the clams; scrub and wash them well. In a pot, add 1 cup of water, a tablespoon of the olive oil and 1 garlic clove. Add the clams, put the heat on medium, cover and leave until all the shells have opened. Clams whose shells have not opened should be discarded. Retain ½ cup of the liquid.

Viareggio is my father's hometown. A beautiful city, it is located on the Tyrrhenian coast, about 12 miles from Lucca. People come from all over Europe to vacation in Viareggio, to enjoy the beautiful beaches, wonderful seafood and the picturesque promenade. A wide variety of the freshest fish can always be found in the fish markets. The fish are brought in at the crack of dawn by the fishermen.

Devein the prawns, leaving the shell on. Clean the calamari bodies and cut them into rings about ½ inch wide, leaving the tentacles whole. Cut the halibut fillets into 2-inch-square pieces.

Chop the onion and sauté in olive oil until the onion begins to become translucent. Add the halibut, prawns and calamari and gently sauté for 3 to 4 minutes over medium heat. Add the chopped parsley, chili pepper and garlic and mix well. Add the white wine and allow to evaporate before adding the peeled, seeded and coarsely chopped tomatoes. Cook on low heat for about 10 minutes. Add the clams and ½ cup of the clam juice, lower the heat and continue to cook for 5 more minutes.

Bring a large pot of salted water to a boil and cook the linguine until *al dente*. Drain the pasta, add the fish sauce and mix well.

Serve immediately.

MEDIUM

PENNE SAPORITE
Penne in a Zesty Tomato Sauce

6   anchovy fillets
4   tablespoons milk
½   cup black olives, chopped
1   garlic clove, minced
2   tablespoons Italian parsley, freshly chopped
½   cup olive oil
½   medium yellow onion, chopped
5   medium tomatoes
2   tablespoons capers
    salt and pepper
1   pound penne

Place the anchovies in a small plate and add the milk. Allow them to soak for 10 minutes to remove most of the excess salt. Then rinse the anchovies. Chop the olives and anchovies and set them aside. Finely chop the garlic and parsley.

Heat the olive oil in a medium sauce pan. Add the chopped onion and sauté for 6 minutes over medium heat. Coarsely chop the tomatoes and add them to the olive oil. Add the parsley, anchovy fillets, olives and capers. Continue to cook over low heat for approximately 12 minutes. Add the salt and pepper as desired. Remember, however, that anchovies tend to be a little salty, so taste the sauce first before adding any salt. Continue to cook for 10 more minutes over low heat.

Cook the pasta until *al dente*, drain and mix well with the sauce.

Capers are pickled and sharp tasting. When combined with anchovies and black olives, they give this pasta a distinct flavor.

Fettuccine di Spinaci con Salsa di Funghi
Spinach Fettuccine with Mushroom Sauce

Although this pasta dish has heavy cream, it has a light and delicate flavor.

1 pound fresh spinach fettuccine
(see page 75 for spinach dough recipe)
1 pound fresh mushrooms
¼ cup Italian parsley, freshly chopped
2 garlic cloves, minced
3 tablespoons olive oil
¼ cup white wine
½ cup heavy cream
½ cup Parmesan cheese, freshly grated
salt

Prepare the fresh spinach fettuccine, set it aside, sprinkle it lightly with flour and allow it to dry for ½ to 1 hour.

Wash and dry the mushrooms and slice them thinly. Chop the parsley and mince the garlic.

In a medium saucepan, allow the olive oil to heat. Then add the mushrooms and gently sauté them for 3 to 4 minutes over medium heat. Add the parsley, garlic and salt. Lower the heat and continue to sauté for 3 to 4 minutes. Add the white wine and cook over low heat until most of the liquid has evaporated.

Cook the pasta until *al dente*. Add the heavy cream to the mushroom sauce and simmer on medium heat for approximately 3 minutes. Add the sauce to the drained pasta. Add the cheese, toss well and serve immediately.

MEDIUM

CONCHIGLIE AI CARCIOFI
Shells with Artichokes

10   small artichokes (found at specialty stores)
      or 1 twelve-ounce package frozen artichokes
½   lemon
½   cup olive oil
1   medium yellow onion, chopped
¼   cup dry white wine
1   teaspoon fresh mint, chopped
3   garlic cloves, minced
    salt
1   pound medium-sized pasta shells,
½   cup Parmesan cheese, freshly grated

Remove the tough outer leaves from the artichokes. Wash the artichokes well and cut them into very thin slices.

Fill a medium-sized bowl with cold water and add the lemon and artichokes. This will prevent the artichokes from becoming discolored.

In a medium sauce pan, heat the olive oil, add the chopped onion and sauté over medium heat for about 5 minutes. Remove the artichokes from the water and dry. Add the sliced artichokes to the olive oil and continue to sauté over medium heat for approximately 10 minutes. Add the wine, mint, minced garlic cloves and salt. Lower heat and cook for another 10 minutes.

In a large pot, bring salted water to a boil and cook the pasta as directed. Drain and then add the pasta to the artichoke sauce and sauté over medium heat for 3 minutes. Add the freshly grated Parmesan cheese, toss and serve.

In Italy, the artichokes are very small, only about 3 inches long, but they are very flavorful. These artichokes can also be used, sliced very thinly, in a salad.

EASY

This quick, easy pasta dish can be made in a few minutes. Remember, however, not to substitute bacon for pancetta because the taste is not at all the same. If pancetta cannot be found, substitute a thick slice of prosciutto.

ORECCHIETTE ALL'AMATRICIANA
Amatriciana-Style Orecchiette

¼ pound pancetta, preferably in 1 thick slice
1 medium yellow onion, chopped
½ cup olive oil
3 large tomatoes, peeled and seeded
   salt
1 teaspoon red hot chili pepper, finely chopped
1 pound orecchiette
½ cup pecorino cheese, grated

Dice the pancetta into small cubes. Finely chop the onion.

Heat the olive oil in a medium-sized pot, add the pancetta and cook for 4 minutes over medium heat. Add the onion and continue to cook for 3 minutes. Add the chopped tomatoes, salt and chopped red hot chili pepper. Continue to cook over low heat for 10 minutes.

Bring a pot of salted water to a boil, add the pasta and cook as directed. Drain the pasta well, toss with the sauce and then add the pecorino cheese.

EASY

TORTELLI DI DIVA
Stuffed Pasta

4 cups meat sauce
  (see page 152 for recipe)
  pasta dough for 8 servings
  (see page 74 for recipe)
1 pound Swiss chard
¾ cup olive oil
4 garlic cloves, minced
2 chicken breasts, boned
1 2-pound pork roast
1 1-pound beef roast

  salt and pepper
2 fresh sage sprigs
1 cup chicken broth
5 bread slices (sourdough)
4 eggs
2 teaspoons fresh thyme
1 teaspoon fresh nutmeg
½ cup dry wine
1 tablespoon parsley, freshly chopped

Bring a large pot of water to boil. Add the cleaned Swiss chard and cook for approximately 8 minutes. Drain well, squeeze out any excess water and finely chop.

Add the olive oil and minced garlic clove to a medium-sized sauce pan. Sauté the Swiss chard over low heat for approximately 3 minutes and put it aside.

Place the chicken, pork roast and beef roast in a large roasting pan. Salt and pepper the meat and add 2 tablespoons of the olive oil to the pan. Add the fresh sage and roast in the oven for approximately 1 hour. (Pork roast may require an additional 10 minutes. If this is so, remove the beef and chicken.) Periodically baste the meats with the wine and pan juices.

Allow the meats to cool. When they have cooled, place them in a food processor and grind them well.

Add the chicken broth and sourdough bread to a medium-sized bowl. Allow the bread to soak in the broth, and then mash the bread well, squeezing out the excess broth. Use only the bread, not the broth.

Combine all the ingredients in a large bowl and mix well. The consistency should be solid. If the mixture does not hold together when spooning, another egg may be added. (Remember, however, that too many eggs can harden the mixture.)

Pasta dough for 8 should be made. The strips should be 5 inches wide. The length depends on whatever is most manageable for you. Place a heaping teaspoon of the mixture in the middle of the strip every 3 inches. Fold the dough over when the strip is completed and cut with a round cutter. Seal each strip with the end of a fork. Place the tortelli on a floured cloth and allow to stand for about 1 hour, turning once.

Bring a large pot with salted water to a boil, add the tortelli, cover and cook over medium heat for 15 minutes. Drain well. Layer the tortelli, freshly grated Parmesan cheese and the meat sauce. Serve hot.

GNOCCHI DI PATATE
Potato Dumplings with Meat Sauce

Gnocchi lend themselves to a variety of different sauces, including tomato, fish or even gorgonzola sauce.

3   cups meat sauce (see page 152 for recipe)
6   medium russet potatoes
2   cups flour
2   teaspoons salt
½   cup Parmesan cheese

Prepare the meat sauce.

Bring a large pot of salted water to a boil. Add the unpeeled potatoes and cook over medium heat for 25 minutes.

On a large pastry board, make a well with the flour. Peel the potatoes. (Hot potatoes give the best results. I find it easier to place a fork in the center of the potato and peel it with a knife). Peel the potatoes and mash them through a ricer into the flour well. Mix the potatoes, flour and salt well, using your hands. Knead the dough until all the flour is absorbed.

Roll the dough into a 1-by-8-inch piece and then cut it into 1-inch cubes (gnocchi) and place them on a floured cloth.

Bring a pot of salted water to a boil. Then add several handfuls of the gnocchi at a time. When the gnocchi are cooked, they will float to the top. Remove the gnocchi with a slotted spoon. In a large bowl, layer the meat sauce, gnocchi and Parmesan cheese.

MEDIUM

LINGUINE CON SALSA AL LIMONE
Linguine with Lemon Sauce

This is a delicate, refreshing pasta dish commonly enjoyed in the summer months.

2 cups milk
5 tablespoons butter
2 tablespoons flour
  salt
1½ lemons
¼ cup Parmesan cheese, freshly grated
1 tablespoon parsley, freshly chopped
1 pound fresh linguine

Bring the milk to a boil. Then set it aside. In a separate pot, melt the butter, add the flour and salt and mix them well. Over low heat, gradually add the hot milk to melted butter and continue to cook over medium heat until the mixture almost comes to a boil and thickens (approximately 10 minutes).

Wash the lemon well. Grate the peel of a whole lemon and half of another. Add the grated peel and Parmesan cheese to the white sauce. Squeeze the lemon juice of ½ lemon, add it to the white sauce and mix well.

Cook the pasta until *al dente*. Drain well and mix with the white sauce. Sprinkle with chopped fresh parsley and lemon rind curls.

RAVIOLI DI SPINACI CON POLLO E RICOTTA
Spinach Ravioli with Chicken and Ricotta

pasta dough for 8 servings
(see page 74 for recipe)
3 cups meat sauce
(see page 152 for recipe)
1 chicken breast, boned
2 tablespoons butter
1 fresh sage sprig
1 pound fresh spinach

1 tablespoon olive oil
30 ounces ricotta cheese
3 egg yolks
1 egg white
1 teaspoon nutmeg
salt and pepper
½ cup Parmesan cheese

Prepare the meat sauce. Sauté the chicken breast in the butter and sage until cooked (about 4 minutes each side). Remove the chicken and finely chop.

Wash and cook the spinach until limp. Squeeze all the excess water from the spinach; then chop it very finely. Heat the olive oil and sauté the spinach over medium heat for approximately 5 minutes. Remove from the heat and set aside.

In a large bowl, mix the ricotta, eggs, nutmeg, salt and pepper. Add the chopped spinach and chicken and mix well.

Stuffed pasta can be prepared in a variety of ways. In Italy, each region has its own special fillings.

Make a basic pasta dough. Place 1 teaspoon of the filling every 2 inches down the center of each strip of the pasta. Fold the sheets in half over the filling, pressing the edges together to seal. Cut with a pastry cutter.

Allow the ravioli to dry for about 30 minutes. Bring a large pot of salted water to a boil and add the ravioli. Cook for 13 minutes over medium heat and drain well when cooked.

Mix the sauce with the ravioli, sprinkle with cheese and serve immediately.

DIFFICULT

PENNE SEMPLICI
Penne in a Simple Sauce

5 medium tomatoes
¼ cup basil, freshly chopped
½ cup parsley, freshly chopped
2 fresh rosemary sprigs
2 garlic cloves, minced
⅓ cup olive oil
½ cup chicken broth
  salt
½ cup pecorino cheese, grated
1 pound penne

Wash, peel, seed and chop the tomatoes finely. Wash and chop the basil, parsley, rosemary and garlic.

Heat the olive oil over low heat, and then add the chopped herbs, cover and sauté over low heat for 5 minutes. Add the tomatoes and chicken broth, stir and cook over low heat for 20 minutes.

In a large pot, bring salted water to a boil. Add the penne noodles and cook until *al dente*. Drain well.

Add the penne noodles to the sauce, mix well and sauté over medium heat for 3 minutes. Place in a serving dish, sprinkle with pecorino cheese and serve immediately.

Fresh rosemary lends a deliciously distinct flavor to this sauce.

LASAGNE VERDI
Spinach Lasagne

    4 cups meat sauce (see page 152 for recipe)
    4 cups béchamel sauce
       (see page 148 for recipe)
       spinach dough for 8 servings
       (see page 75 for recipe)
    1 cup Parmesan cheese, freshly grated
    2 tablespoons butter
   ½ cup chicken broth

Prepare the meat sauce and the béchamel sauce. Make the spinach dough and cut it into pasta sheets to fit a 9-by-13-inch baking dish. Dry pasta sheets for 20 minutes. Bring a large pot of salted water to a boil, add 5 to 6 pasta sheets and cook for 1 minute. Remove pasta sheets with a slotted spoon and lay them on a cloth towel. Repeat this process with the remaining pasta sheets.

Layer the lasagne noodles in a baking dish, beginning first with the meat sauce, then the pasta sheets, then the white sauce and the cheese. Continue this process for about 5 layers. Sprinkle on the remaining Parmesan cheese and dot with the remaining butter.

Cover the dish with aluminum foil and bake at 350 degrees for 25 minutes. Then uncover the dish and cook for 10 more minutes. If the pasta seems dry, add several tablespoons of chicken broth.

Allow the lasagne to stand for about 5 minutes before cutting and serving.

 MEDIUM

Here is another pasta dish offering a delicious combination of meat and white sauces. This lasagne truly is a specialty.

*Il mangiare insegna
a lavorare.*
(Eating teaches you to work.)

PENNE AL FORNO
Baked Penne Noodles
with Red and White Sauce

4   cups pomarola sauce
    (see page 150 for recipe)
3   cups béchamel sauce
    (see page 148 for recipe)
⅔   cup Parmesan cheese, freshly grated
2   tablespoons butter
1   pound penne
1   cup chicken broth
    salt

Prepare the pomarola sauce and the béchamel sauce. Bring a large pot of salted water to a boil and cook the pasta until *al dente*.

Drain the pasta well and combine with the pomarola and béchamel sauces. Add cheese and mix well.

Butter a large baking dish. Add the penne and the sauces, cover the baking dish with aluminum foil and bake at 350 degrees for 35 minutes. Periodically pour a small amount of broth over the penne to keep the pasta moist.

 MEDIUM

This is a delicate and delicious dish that can be prepared several hours in advance.

VARIATION
A meat sauce can be substituted for the tomato sauce. See page 152 for recipe.

Sage is an herb featured in many Italian dishes. It grows wild in the hills around Lucca and lends a distinctly classical flavor when combined with olive oil and butter to season pasta.

FETTUCCINE ALLA SALVIA FRESCA
Fettuccine with Fresh Sage

20 sage leaves, freshly chopped
3 garlic cloves, minced
½ cup olive oil
2 tablespoons butter
1 pound fettuccine
½ cup pecorino cheese, grated
  salt

Coarsely chop the sage and mince the garlic. In a small pan, heat the olive oil, butter, sage and garlic and cook for about 3 minutes over low heat. Do not let the garlic brown or the sage burn.

Bring a large pot of salted water to a boil and cook the fettucine until *al dente*. Drain the pasta well. Combine the pasta with the sauce and pecorino cheese. Garnish with fresh sage sprigs.

FARFALLE ALLE VERDURE
Butterfly Pasta with Vegetables

A modest way of serving pasta, but simply delicious.

2   carrots
2   celery stalks
1   medium red onion
¼   cup Italian parsley, freshly chopped
¼   cup basil, freshly chopped
2   garlic cloves, minced
⅓   cup olive oil
5   tomatoes
    salt
1   pound farfalle
½   cup Parmesan cheese, freshly grated

Dice the carrots, celery stalks and onion. Chop the parsley and basil and mince the garlic.

In a medium-sized pot, heat the olive oil, add the carrots, celery and onion. Cook on low heat for about 10 minutes.

Peel and seed the tomatoes, and chop coarsely. Add them to the pot and cook for 5 minutes. Add the chopped parsley, salt, basil and garlic and continue to cook for 20 minutes on low heat.

Bring a large pot of salted water to a boil and cook the farfalle until *al dente*.

Mix the sauce with the noodles, add cheese and serve.

Gorgonzola can be found in mild and strong varieties.

SPAGHETTI AL GORGONZOLA
Spaghetti with Gorgonzola Cheese

16 ounces spaghetti
 3 tablespoons butter
¾ cup light cream
 4 ounces gorgonzola cheese
 1 tablespoon salt
    fresh pepper

Cook the spaghetti in boiling salted water.

Heat the butter, light cream and gorgonzola in a double boiler. Stir continuously, and do not allow the sauce to boil. When the sauce is smooth and well blended, remove it from the heat.

When the pasta is cooked, drain it well and mix the sauce with the spaghetti. Mix well so that the sauce coats the spaghetti evenly. Sprinkle with fresh ground pepper.

This pasta should be served very hot.

ORECCHIETTE CON SPINACI E RICOTTA
Little Ears with Spinach and Ricotta

½   pound fresh spinach
1   pound orecchiette
2   tablespoons butter
3   tablespoons olive oil
1   15-ounce container of
     whole milk ricotta cheese
¼   cup Parmesan cheese, grated
2   tablespoons salt
½   teaspoon nutmeg

Wash the spinach and trim and discard the stems. In a large pot, bring 4 cups of water to a boil. Add the spinach, cover it and cook for about 10 minutes. When the spinach is cooked, squeeze it and drain the excess water. Place the spinach in a food processor and puree.

Cook the pasta in a large pot of salted boiling water. In a smaller pot, melt the butter and add the olive oil and the pureed spinach. Sauté over low heat for 3 to 4 minutes. Add the ricotta cheese, Parmesan cheese, nutmeg and salt and combine well. When the pasta is cooked and drained, mix well with the spinach sauce and serve immediately.

 MEDIUM

I recently had lunch at a wonderful little restaurant in Florence with my two cousins. This is where I discovered this unique pasta dish. The gentleman next to me was served a delicious-smelling pasta, so I decided to order the same. It was absolutely delightful.

CANNELLONI DI RICOTTA E SPINACI
Stuffed Cannelloni with Ricotta and Spinach

basic pasta dough for 8 servings (see page 74 for recipe)	30 ounces ricotta cheese
4 cups béchamel sauce (see page 148 for recipe)	2 eggs
	1 pound fresh spinach
4 cups meat sauce (see page 152 for recipe)	½ cup Parmesan cheese
	1 tablespoon parsley, freshly chopped
	salt

Prepare the béchamel and meat sauce.

Wash and trim the spinach, discarding the stems. Cook the spinach in plenty of water, drain, squeeze the excess water out and finely chop.

In a large bowl, place the ricotta, eggs, spinach, Parmesan cheese, parsley and salt and combine well.

Prepare the pasta dough and cut the sheets into 4-inch squares. Bring a large pot of salted water to a boil and cook the 5 or 6 pasta squares for 1 minute. Remove the pasta squares with a slotted spoon and place them on a cloth towel. Repeat this process with the remaining pasta squares.

Cannelloni also can be filled with meats or fish. This spinach and ricotta version is lighter and perfect for lunch or summer meals.

Place 1 tablespoon of the filling in the center of each pasta square and fold the pasta over the filling to make a tube. Continue this process until all the pasta squares are done.

Cover the bottom of a 9-by-13-inch baking dish with the meat sauce. Place the cannelloni with the folded edges down, then a layer of béchamel sauce, then a layer of meat sauce, and repeat this process until all the cannelloni have been layered. Sprinkle with Parmesan cheese.

Preheat oven to 375 degrees and bake for 30 minutes.

 DIFFICULT

LASAGNE AI FUNGHI
Lasagne with Mushroom Sauce

4 cups béchamel sauce
  (see page 148 for recipe)
  basic pasta dough for 8 servings
  (see page 74 for recipe)
2 ounces dried porcini mushrooms
½ pound fresh white mushrooms
½ pound mixed mushrooms
  (for instance, shiitake, porta bella)
½ cup olive oil

2 tablespoons butter
3 garlic cloves, minced
½ cup dry white wine
2 tablespoons parsley,
  freshly chopped
  salt
1 cup Parmesan cheese,
  freshly grated
½ cup chicken broth

Prepare the béchamel sauce.

Soak the porcini mushrooms in 1 cup of hot water for 20 minutes. Remove the porcini mushrooms, retain the liquid and finely chop the mushrooms. Wash, dry and thinly slice the other mushrooms.

In a large skillet, heat the olive oil and butter and add chopped garlic. Sauté the garlic over low heat for 2 minutes. Add the sliced mushrooms and continue to sauté for 5 minutes. Add the porcini mushrooms, white wine, parsley and salt and continue to cook for 15 more minutes.

Prepare the pasta dough for a 9-by-13-inch baking dish. Dry the pasta sheets for 20 minutes. Bring a large pot of salted water to a boil, add 5 to 6 pasta sheets and cook for about 1 minute. Remove the pasta sheets with a slotted spoon and lay them on a cloth towel. Repeat this process with the remaining pasta sheets.

Cover the bottom of the baking dish with the mushroom sauce, then a layer of the pasta and white sauce and sprinkle with Parmesan cheese. Repeat this process for 4 layers, ending with the mushroom sauce. Sprinkle with freshly grated Parmesan cheese.

Bake at 350 degrees for 35 minutes. If the lasagne seems dry, add a small amount of chicken broth while the lasagne is baking.

Allow to stand for 5 minutes before cutting and serving.

> This lasagne dish is a nice change from the traditional lasagne. It is a bit lighter than the lasagne most people are familiar with.

DIFFICULT

This pasta dish has a distinct flavor because of the smoked salmon.

PENNE AL SALMONE AFFUMICATO
Penne with Smoked Salmon

½ cup olive oil
2 garlic cloves, minced
6 ounces smoked sliced salmon
1 teaspoon lemon peel, grated
½ cup dry white wine
    salt
1 teaspoon red hot chili pepper,
    finely chopped
¼ cup parsley, freshly chopped
1 pound penne

In a medium saucepan, heat the olive oil and sauté the garlic for 2 minutes over low heat. Cut the smoked salmon into 1-inch pieces. Add the salmon, lemon peel, white wine, salt and chili pepper and sauté for 3 minutes over medium heat.

Add the parsley and continue to sauté until the wine has evaporated.

Cook the pasta until *al dente* and drain well. Return the pasta to the pot, add the salmon sauce and sauté the pasta for 2 minutes over medium heat. Place the pasta in a serving dish and enjoy.

TAGLIATELLE CON ZUCCHINE
Tagliatelle with Zucchini

4	small to medium zucchini
1	small red onion, chopped
½	cup olive oil
1	tablespoon mint, chopped
	salt
¼	cup white wine
16	ounces tagliatelle
½	cup pecorino cheese, freshly grated

Thinly slice the zucchini and finely chop the onion.

Heat the olive oil and sauté the onion in a medium-sized sauce pan over low heat until translucent. Add the zucchini and mint and continue to cook for 5 minutes. Add the salt and wine and continue to cook until the wine has evaporated (about 10 minutes).

Cook the pasta until *al dente* and drain well. Add the zucchini sauce and freshly grated pecorino cheese, mix well and serve immediately.

This sauce is best made during the summer months with the freshest zucchini. Also, keep in mind that the smaller the zucchini, the more flavorful they are.

TYPES OF PASTA

CANNELLONI
Pasta that is similar in shape to a tube and is generally filled with either a meat or spinach-and-cheese filling. Usually an egg pasta.

CAPELLINI
A very fine spaghetti. The literal meaning is "fine hair."

CONCHIGLIE
This is a shell-like pasta. Typically used in pasta dishes with a sauce, they are about 1¼ inches long and come in several sizes.

FARFALLE
Means "butterflies." This pasta has a shape very similar to that of a butterfly.

FETTUCCINE
This is a thin, ribbonlike pasta. About ¼ of an inch wide, fettucine is easy to make at home and also can be store bought. Usually an egg pasta.

FUSILLI
This pasta is shaped like a spring.

LASAGNE
These are large squares or rectangles of pasta, typically layered with sauces, then baked. Usually an egg pasta.

(continued)

PASTA ALL' UOVO
Egg Pasta Dough

| Ingredients needed: | Flour | | |
| | Eggs | | |

To make:	4 servings	6 servings	8 servings
Flour	2 cups	3 cups	4½ cups
Eggs	3	4	6

On a pastry board, pour the flour and make a well. Then break the eggs into the well and beat them with a fork. Continually draw some of the flour from the well over the eggs, consistently beating with the fork.

Remove the pieces of dough attached to the pastry board.

Lightly flour the pastry board. Knead the dough for about 10 minutes, adding flour if needed until the dough is smooth and pliable.

Set the rollers on your pasta machine at their widest. Cut small pieces of dough about the size of an egg. Cover the remaining dough with a cloth. Flatten out the egg-sized piece of dough, dust it with flour and run it through the pasta machine. Fold the pasta in half. This step should be repeated 4 to 5 times until the dough is smooth.

Change the width notches on your pasta machine to the next setting, and repeat the steps above. Continue to change the settings until the pasta is the desired thickness.

Remember to dust the pasta with flour between runs through the machine.

Pasta Verde
Spinach Pasta Dough

Ingredients needed: Flour
                                   Eggs
                                   Spinach

To make:	4 servings	6 servings	8 servings
Spinach	⅓ cup cooked and chopped	½ cup cooked and chopped	⅔ cup cooked and chopped
Flour	2 cups	3 cups	4 cups
Eggs	2	3	4

Cook the spinach according to the instructions on the package. After the spinach is cooked, drain it thoroughly and squeeze it to remove all moisture.

Chop the spinach finely. Place the flour on the pastry board, make a well and break the eggs into it. Beat the eggs with a fork, add the chopped spinach and continue to beat to combine. Follow the same steps as for the egg pasta dough.

LINGUINE
This is also a flat, ribbonlike pasta, only a smaller version of fettucine. *Linguine* means "little tongues."

MACCHERONI
A flat 2-inch-square pasta. Usually an egg pasta.

ORECCHIETTE
Literally means "little ears." Best if made at home, but also can be store bought.

PASTINA
This name is given to very small pasta usually used in soups.

PENNE
This is a short tubular pasta that is cut diagonally at both ends.

RIGATONI
This is a short, wide tubular pasta about 1¼ inches long with a ribbed surface.

SPAGHETTI
Everyone should know what type of pasta this is!

TAGLIATELLE
Similar to fettucine. If store bought, they are frequently found in round nests. This is an egg pasta.

TRENETTE
These noodles are about ⅛ inch wide and are long and flat, like ribbons.

SECONDI

BEEF
PORK
LAMB
POULTRY
FISH

Literally meaning "the second" course, *i secondi* is formally referred to as the main course and typically consists of meat, veal, pork, lamb, chicken or fish. It can be stewed, sautéed, roasted or grilled. Generally, this course is served with vegetables. Many times in Italy, an antipasto dish and a *secondo* will be ordered, but not a *primo*. The second course can be a delicate fish dish or a hearty beef stew. In Italy, the portions of the various courses are usually not overfilling. There are so many different courses, so a little of each goes a long way.

Anchovies and capers give this scaloppine dish its Tuscan flavor.

SCALOPPINE ALLA TOSCANA
Tuscany-Style Scaloppine

1 egg
3 tablespoons butter
½ cup olive oil
1 pound thinly sliced beef (sirloin is very good to use; ask your butcher for a slice of beef from a sirloin roast)
½ cup flour
3 tablespoons marsala wine
  salt
4 tablespoons tomato sauce
½ cup broth
6 anchovy fillets
1 tablespoon capers

Beat the egg in a small bowl. Heat the butter and olive oil in a large pan. Dredge slices of the beef first in flour, then in the egg, and fry in the olive oil until they are golden brown on both sides. When the meat has browned on both sides, use the marsala wine to deglaze the pan. Add salt to taste and simmer until the marsala has evaporated. Remove the meat from the pan and set it aside.

In the same pan, add the tomato sauce diluted in ½ cup of the broth and simmer over low heat for 10 minutes. Add the chopped anchovies and capers and continue to cook for 3 minutes. Add the sliced meat to the sauce and cook for 5 minutes.

 MEDIUM

VARIATION
Add sliced mushrooms to the sauce when adding broth.

ROVELLINE (BRACIOLE) DI MIA MADRE
Sliced Beef in Tomato Sauce

This is an all-time favorite with my family and friends. The sauce has a uniquely tangy flavor.

12   slices beef (sirloin or eye of round roast can be used easily)
 2   eggs
     salt and pepper
 1   cup bread crumbs
     light olive oil for frying
 ½   cup olive oil
 ⅓   cup parsley, freshly chopped
 ½   carrot, finely chopped
 ½   onion, finely chopped
 1   garlic clove, minced
 1   teaspoon lemon rind, finely chopped
 ⅔   cup tomato sauce
 2   tablespoons capers
 ¼   cup chicken broth

Place the meat between 2 pieces of waxed paper and pound it until it is thin. In a bowl, beat the eggs, salt and pepper. Dip the slices of the beef in the egg and then coat with the bread crumbs.

In a frying pan, heat the olive oil and fry each piece of meat until golden brown on each side. Place the meat on paper towels to soak up any excess oil. Set it aside.

Finely chop the parsley, carrot, onion, garlic and lemon rind. In a large pan, heat the olive oil and add the chopped vegetables and lemon rind. Sauté over medium heat for about 10 minutes. Add the tomato sauce and continue to simmer for about 5 minutes. Add the capers and broth and cook on low heat for 15 minutes.

When the sauce is cooked, add the slices of beef, cook over low heat for 5 minutes and serve immediately.

VARIATION

Add sliced mushrooms or olives to the sauce when the tomato sauce is added. Also, instead of using beef, thin slices of chicken can be substituted.

 MEDIUM

79

This dish makes for a quick
and easy meal.

Fette di Manzo al Formaggio e Marsala
Beef with Marsala and Cheese

10 small beef cutlets (thin slices of sirloin or eye
of round can be used)
⅔ cup flour
¼ cup olive oil
3 tablespoons butter
⅓ cup marsala wine
salt
10 slices of Italian fontina cheese

Coat the cutlets in flour. Heat the olive oil and butter in a large
pan. Add the cutlets and cook on each side for 2 minutes on
medium heat. Add the marsala wine and salt the cutlets. Allow to
cook until some of the wine has evaporated (about 4 minutes).

Place 1 slice of fontina cheese on each cutlet, cover for 2 minutes
and serve immediately.

Ossobuco Capezzano
Veal or Beef Shanks

4   veal or beef shanks (about 1½ inches thick)
    flour
1   onion, finely chopped
1   carrot, finely chopped
1   celery stalk, finely chopped
½   cup olive oil
½   cup parsley, freshly chopped
¼   cup tomato sauce
4   cups broth
1   cup warm water
    salt and pepper

Coat the shanks with flour and set aside. Chop the onion, carrot and celery stalk. In a large pan, heat the olive oil and brown the shanks over medium heat on each side for about 3 minutes. Remove the shanks and set aside.

In the same pan, add the chopped vegetables and parsley, allowing them to cook over low heat for about 15 minutes. Add the tomato sauce and cook for 5 minutes. Add the beef shanks, broth and 1 cup of water. The meat should be covered with liquid. Cover and cook on low heat for 2 hours. Allow the meat to cook uncovered for another 10 minutes or until the liquid has evaporated and the sauce has thickened.

 MEDIUM

When the ossobuco is cooked, I sometimes remove about 3 tablespoons of sauce and make a risotto, thus creating two dishes in one.

SALTIMBOCCA ALLA LUCCHESE
Lucca-Style Cutlets

This dish is an elegant staple of fine Tuscan tables. *Saltimbocca* literally means "jump in the mouth," a reference to its exquisite taste.

salt and pepper
8 thin slices cooked ham
8 fresh sage leaves
8 beef cutlets
4 tablespoons butter
½ cup white wine
¼ cup chicken broth

Salt and pepper each cutlet. Lay 1 slice of the ham and 1 sage leaf on each cutlet and secure with a toothpick, leaving the meat flat.

Heat the butter in a large skillet and brown the meat. Add the white wine and cook until the liquid is reduced to 2 tablespoons. Cover and cook over low heat for 10 minutes, adding a little broth so that the meat does not dry out. Serve immediately.

STUFATO DI MANZO
Beef Stew

½	cup olive oil
1½	pounds stew meat cut into 2-inch-square pieces
4	medium potatoes
3	celery stalks
1	medium onion
3	carrots
1	cup fresh peas or 1 ten-ounce package frozen peas
¾	cup tomato sauce
1	cup chicken broth
½	cup water
	salt and pepper

Heat the olive oil in a large skillet and brown the meat well on both sides. Remove the meat and set it aside. Cut the potatoes, celery, onion and carrots into 1-inch pieces.

In the same skillet, place all the cut vegetables and sauté them for about 5 minutes. Add the cooked meat, the tomato sauce, 1 cup of broth, ½ cup water, salt and pepper. Cover and cook over low heat for about 1 hour. Uncover the skillet the last 10 minutes to allow some of the liquid to evaporate.

 MEDIUM

This is a great meal for a cold, wintery night. A loaf of Italian bread, stew and a good bottle of red wine is all you need for a complete meal.

INVOLTINI DI MANZO
Little Stuffed Meat Rolls

12	thin slices beef (sirloin, eye of round)
8	sage leaves, chopped
1	garlic clove, minced
	salt and pepper
½	cup olive oil
¼	cup tomato sauce
¼	cup white wine
¼	cup chicken broth
½	pint olives (green Italian olives or dried black olives)

Place the beef between 2 sheets of waxed paper and pound it until it is flattened. Chop the sage and garlic finely. Salt and pepper each slice of beef and then spread with a very small amount of the herb mixture. Roll the meat and either tie the roll with a string or secure it with a toothpick.

In a skillet, heat the olive oil and brown the meat on both sides. When the meat is browned, turn the heat to low and add the tomato sauce, ¼ cup of wine and the chicken broth and cook uncovered for 15 minutes. Add the olives and continue to cook over low heat for 10 more minutes or until the liquid is reduced to 3 tablespoons.

Remove the string or toothpicks before serving.

 MEDIUM

SCALOPPINE DI VITELLA AL LIMONE
Veal Scaloppine with Lemon Sauce

¼   cup olive oil
4   tablespoons butter
1¼   pound veal scaloppine
¾   cup flour
1½   lemons, juice only
     salt and pepper
1   garlic clove, minced
¼   cup parsley, freshly chopped

Heat the olive oil and butter in a large skillet. Coat the scaloppine in flour and add it to the skillet. Cook for 2 minutes, turn the meat and cook for 2 additional minutes. Add the lemon juice, salt, pepper, garlic and parsley and continue to cook over low heat for 3 minutes.

Remove from heat and serve hot.

Scaloppine is a classic dish common to the tables of Northern Italy. Noted for its lighter sauces, Tuscan cooking often uses fresh lemon, as in this version, to enhance the flavor of veal.

The first time I ate tagliata was at my cousin's restaurant in Lucca. It seemed like an odd way to serve beef, topped with a sort of raw lettuce, but the flavor of the arugula leaves combined with beef produces a startling, charming dish.

TAGLIATA ALLA RUCOLA
Broiled Beef with Arugula

2	pounds London broil
½	cup olive oil
2	lemons, juice only
½	pound fresh arugula leaves
	salt and pepper

In a small bowl, whisk the olive oil, lemon juice, salt and freshly ground pepper. Set aside. Wash and dry the arugula leaves and chop them finely.

Broil the meat to the desired wellness (about 6 to 8 minutes on each side for medium wellness). When the meat is cooked, slice it thinly and place the slices on a serving platter.

Place the chopped arugula over the top of the sliced meat, pour the sauce evenly over the top and serve immediately.

EASY

ARROSTO DI VITELLA
Veal Roast

2	garlic cloves, minced
2½	pounds veal roast
	salt and pepper
4	prosciutto slices, thinly cut
2	rosemary sprigs
¼	cup olive oil plus 1 tablespoon
1½	cups dry white wine

Slice each garlic clove into three sections. Make 6 small slits in the veal roast and tuck a sliver of garlic and a pinch of salt and pepper into each slit.

Cover the roast with the prosciutto slices, place 1 rosemary sprig on the top and bottom of the veal roast and secure the roast tightly with string.

Place the olive oil and roast in a deep pot. Brown the roast on both sides for 6 minutes over medium heat. Lower the heat and add ¼ cup of water, continuing to add the wine to flavor the roast and keep it moist. The roast should cook for 1½ hours and should always be kept moist. Continue to add more liquid if needed.

Slice the roast and arrange on a platter, pour the juices over the roast and serve.

 MEDIUM

As the roast cooks, it will fill your kitchen with an unforgettable aroma reminiscent of some of the best kitchens in Lucca.

The fresh rosemary adds an
excellent flavor to this roast.

ARROSTO DI MAIALE
Pork Loin Roast

6   fresh rosemary sprigs, finely chopped
4   garlic cloves, minced
¼   cup olive oil
    salt and pepper
1   3-pound pork loin roast
⅔   cup white wine

Wash and dry the rosemary. Finely chop 4 sprigs of rosemary
and the garlic. In a small bowl, mix 1 tablespoon of the olive oil,
minced garlic and rosemary and add 1 teaspoon of salt and
pepper.

Make about 6 slits in the roast about 1 inch deep, and fill each slit
with a teaspoon of the mixture. Rub any extra herb mixture that
remains on the outside of the roast. Place the remaining rosemary
on the bottom and the top of the roast.

In a roasting pan, add the remaining olive oil and the pork loin
roast. Place in an oven preheated to 375 degrees and roast for
about 1 hour and 45 minutes. Periodically baste the pork loin
with the wine.

When roast is cooked, slice and place on serving platter.

VARIATION
When the roast has cooked
for 1 hour, add potatoes that
have been peeled and cut. Then
continue to cook for 1 more
hour to allow the potatoes to
absorb the flavor of the roast.

SPIEDINI DI MAIALE
Broiled Pork Skewers

2 pounds pork loin
3 fresh rosemary sprigs, chopped
3 garlic cloves, minced
6 slices coarse bread
½ pound sliced pancetta,
    cut into about 4 thick pieces
½ cup olive oil
2 cups white wine
    salt and pepper

Cut the pork into 2-inch squares. Chop the rosemary and mince the garlic. Slice the bread and cut the pancetta into 2-inch squares.

In a bowl, combine the olive oil, rosemary, garlic, wine, salt and pepper. Add the cubed pork to the marinade and refrigerate it for at least 6 hours. Drain the pork cubes on paper towels and retain the marinade. Drizzle each slice of bread with a little olive oil on each side.

Alternate the pork, bread and pancetta on the skewers. Broil for 6 minutes on each side, periodically brushing with the remaining marinade.

This delicious pork dish is relatively easy to make. Pancetta gives these skewers their unique flavor.

VARIATION
These skewers are also wonderful when barbecued. Vegetables such as onions, red bell peppers or zucchini also can be cut and added to the skewers.

INVOLTINI DI MAIALE
Pork Bundles

10 slices boneless tenderloin pork
 2 sprigs fresh rosemary, finely chopped
¼ cup olive oil plus 1 tablespoon
20 salt-cured olives
¼ pound prosciutto (10 very thin slices)
 2 tablespoons butter
    salt and pepper
¾ cup dry white wine

Lay the slices of pork between waxed paper and pound them until they are fairly thin. Chop the rosemary very finely and add 1 tablespoon of the olive oil, mixing well. Chop the olives coarsely.

Place 1 slice of the prosciutto, a pinch of the rosemary mixture and a pinch of the chopped olives over each slice of pork. Roll up the pork and secure with 2 wooden toothpicks.

In a medium skillet, melt the butter and the remaining olive oil. Add the pork bundles and brown them on each side. Season them with salt and pepper, add the wine and continue to cook them over low heat for 20 minutes or until most of the wine has evaporated.

Serve the pork bundles with the remaining sauce poured over them.

 MEDIUM

This is an appetizing way to serve pork. The olives give this pork dish a flavorful combination of tastes.

ARROSTO DI MAIALE AL LATTE
Pork Loin Roast Braised in Milk

2   pounds pork loin roast
3   cups dry white wine
3   tablespoons butter
    salt
    freshly ground pepper
4   cups milk
3   rosemary sprigs
3   sage leaves

Marinate the roast in white wine for at least 12 hours. Remove the roast from the marinade and pat dry.

In a large pot, heat the butter, add the pork roast, salt and pepper and cook for 10 minutes, turning the roast once in the pot. Add the milk, rosemary sprigs and sage leaves and simmer over low heat for 1½ hours.

Remove the roast from the pot, slice it and arrange it on a platter. Strain the milk sauce and pour it over the sliced pork roast.

This is a classic braised pork dish of the Tuscany region. The milk sauce served over the pork is typical of the delicate, herbed sauces common to this region.

This is a quick meal for those evenings when unexpected guests arrive.

BISTECCHINE DI MAIALE
Pork Chops in White Wine

2 garlic cloves, minced
1 tablespoon rosemary, freshly chopped
  salt and pepper
  pinch red hot chili pepper, finely chopped
6 pork chops, 1 inch thick
3 tablespoons olive oil
½ cup dry white wine
¼ cup chicken broth

In a small bowl, combine the garlic, rosemary, salt, pepper and chili. Gently rub the pork chops on each side with the mixture.

In a large skillet, heat the olive oil, add the pork chops and brown them on both sides and then add the white wine. When the wine has evaporated, add the chicken broth, cover and cook over low heat until most of the broth has evaporated (about 10 minutes).

VARIATION
Add ½ pound of sliced mushrooms when adding the white wine.

SPEZZATINO DI AGNELLO
Lamb with Olives

This lamb dish is a specialty in Lucca. The dried, cured olives give the lamb a distinct flavor.

½ cup olive oil
2 pounds lean lamb, cubed (1 to 2 inches)
3 garlic cloves, minced
1 tablespoon rosemary, finely chopped
3 tablespoons tomato sauce
¾ cup dry white wine
½ pint black olives (salt-cured olives
   traditionally are used in this dish,
   although any olive can be used)
   salt and pepper

Heat the olive oil in a large pan. Add the lamb and cook over medium heat until the lamb is browned on each side (approximately 5 to 8 minutes).

Finely chop the garlic and rosemary. Lower the heat and add the chopped herbs to the lamb. Mix the tomato sauce in with the wine and add to the lamb. Cook over low heat for 15 minutes. Add the olives and simmer on low heat for 20 more minutes. Remove from heat and serve.

COSTOLETTE D'AGNELLO ARROSTO
Roasted Rack of Lamb with Herbs and Wine

Roasted lamb with garlic and rosemary is a classic way to prepare this dish.

6 fresh rosemary sprigs, finely chopped
4 garlic cloves, minced
½ cup olive oil
   salt and pepper
1 3-pound rack of lamb
1 cup red wine

Finely chop the rosemary and garlic. In a small bowl, add 2 tablespoons of the olive oil, salt, pepper and chopped herbs and mix well.

Make small slits in the rack of lamb and tuck a small amount of the herb mixture in each slit. Brush the remaining herb mixture over the rack of lamb.

In a large roasting pan, add the remaining olive oil and lamb. Preheat the oven to 400 degrees, allow the lamb to brown for about 10 minutes on each side and then turn the oven down to 350 degrees. As the lamb is turned, add ¼ cup of the wine. Cook at 350 degrees for approximately 45 minutes. Periodically baste the lamb with the remaining wine.

Slice each lamb chop before serving.

La meglio carne sta attaccata all'osso.
(The sweetest meat is attached to the bone.)

COSTOLETTE D'AGNELLO
Broiled Lamb Chops

3 garlic cloves, minced
2 tablespoons Italian parsley, chopped
3 fresh rosemary sprigs, chopped
¾ cup red wine
¼ cup olive oil
   salt and pepper
6 1½-inch-thick lamb chops

Finely chop 2 garlic cloves, the parsley and the rosemary. In a small bowl, combine the red wine, olive oil, salt, pepper and chopped herbs. Mix well.

Slice the remaining garlic clove into 6 slices. Make a small slit in each lamb chop and insert a garlic clove slice. Place the lamb chops on a broiler pan and pour 1 teaspoon of the wine/herb sauce on each lamb chop. Broil the lamb chops approximately 4 minutes on each side. As they brown, add the wine/herb sauce.

Sautéed greens go well with this lamb dish.

COSTOLETTE DI AGNELLO FRITTE
Fried Lamb Chops

Tuscans love to eat these small lamb chops fried and served with a mixed green salad.

8	thin lamb chops
½	cup flour
1	teaspoon salt
¼	teaspoon pepper
½	cup bread crumbs
1	teaspoon rosemary, freshly chopped
1	egg
2	tablespoons warm water
1	cup light olive oil
2	lemons, cut into wedges

The lamb chops should be sliced no more than ½ of an inch thick.

In a bowl, combine the flour, salt and pepper and set aside. In another bowl, combine the bread crumbs, rosemary, egg and water and mix well.

Preheat the olive oil in a large skillet. Dredge each lamb chop in flour and then gently pat each lamb chop with the bread crumb mixture, ensuring that each lamb chop is well coated on both sides. The olive oil should be kept on medium heat. Place the lamb chops in the olive oil and fry them for approximately 3 minutes on each side or until they are golden brown. Place the cooked chops on a warm platter and serve them immediately. Garnish with lemon wedges. (Fresh lemon juice enhances the flavor of lamb.)

 MEDIUM

POLLO ARROSTO AL LIMONE
Roasted Lemon Chicken

1   3½-pound whole chicken
1   chicken bouillon cube
3   tablespoons butter
2   garlic cloves
3   fresh rosemary sprigs
1   teaspoon salt
1   teaspoon pepper
2   lemons, cut into quarters

Wash the chicken thoroughly inside and out and dry it completely. Place the bouillon cube, 1 tablespoon of butter, garlic cloves, rosemary sprigs and 2 lemon quarters inside the chicken.

Sprinkle salt and pepper on the outside of the chicken and make sure the chicken's legs are tied together to keep the flavoring inside.

Place the chicken, the remaining 2 tablespoons of butter and the other remaining lemon quarters in a roaster pan. Roast at 375 degrees for approximately 1½ hours, basting occasionally with juices. When chicken is cooked, cut into quarters and serve.

The lemon and fresh rosemary give this roasted chicken dish a truly excellent flavor. The chicken remains moist, with a hint of lemon.

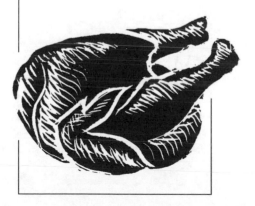

In Lucca, this chicken dish often is accompanied by polenta as a traditional winter meal.

POLLO IN UMIDO
Chicken in Tomato and Olive Sauce

1	3-pound chicken, cut into pieces
⅔	cup olive oil
¾	cup white wine
½	medium yellow onion, diced
2	garlic cloves, minced
5	fresh sage leaves, chopped
	salt and pepper
1	cup tomato sauce
⅔	cup chicken broth
1	pint black olives

Wash the chicken thoroughly inside and out and dry it completely. Cut the chicken into small pieces (e.g., from 1 chicken breast, cut 3 pieces).

On medium heat, prepare a large skillet with the olive oil. When the oil is hot, add the chicken. Sauté the chicken on medium heat until it is browned well on both sides (approximately 10 minutes). Remove the chicken and set it aside. In the same skillet, add the wine, minced herbs and onion. Allow to simmer for 5 minutes. Then add the salt, pepper, tomato sauce and broth.

Allow to cook over medium heat until the liquid begins to evaporate (approximately 15 minutes). Add the chicken and olives to the sauce and continue to cook on low heat for ½ hour or until the sauce has thickened. Place the chicken on a serving dish and pour the remaining sauce over the chicken.

MEDIUM

VARIATION
Black dried olives or green Italian olives will give this chicken a wonderful flavor. You can also substitute the olives with about ½ pound of sliced fresh mushrooms.

POLLO CON MARSALA E FUNGHI
Chicken Marsala with Mushrooms

This chicken dish is particularly popular with my guests. I learned this recipe from friends many years ago while living in Italy.

2	whole chicken breast fillets
½	cup of flour
½	cup olive oil
	salt and pepper
½	teaspoon lemon rind, minced
2	garlic cloves, minced
¼	cup parsley, chopped
½	cup dry white wine
½	cup dry marsala dry wine
½	pound fresh mushrooms

Thinly slice each chicken breast (for example, from 1 chicken breast, cut 3 slices). Lay each slice between 2 pieces of waxed paper and pound it so that the chicken is thin and similar to a cutlet. Flour each slice.

Heat the olive oil in a large skillet; add the chicken breasts, salt, and pepper; and cook on medium heat for about 3 minutes on each side. Then add lemon rind, garlic and parsley and cook on low heat for an additional 2 minutes. Add the white wine, marsala and sliced mushrooms. Stir gently to combine the mushrooms and chicken. Continue to cook for 15 minutes. Remove from heat and serve.

MEDIUM

Fungo buono non nasce mai solo.
(Good mushrooms never grow by themselves.)

Some of the tastiest chickens
come from the Tuscany region,
where many are raised
"free range."

INVOLTINI DI POLLO
Stuffed Chicken Breasts

2	whole chicken breasts, boned and skinned
10	fresh sage leaves, chopped
2	cloves garlic, minced
½	cup olive oil
8	thin slices of prosciutto
½	cup dry white wine
	salt and pepper

Wash the chicken and pat it dry. Each chicken breast should be
sliced into approximately 3 pieces, and each slice should be
placed between waxed paper and pounded.

Finely chop the sage and garlic. Then add 1 teaspoon of olive oil
and mix well. Lay each chicken piece flat, place a small slice of
prosciutto on the chicken, just enough to cover the slice, and add
a pinch of the herb mixture. Roll the chicken so that the mixture
and prosciutto remain enclosed, and seal each slice with a
toothpick.

In a large skillet, preheat the olive oil and brown the chicken over
medium heat, about 4 minutes on each side. When the chicken is
browned, add the wine, salt, pepper and remaining herb mixture.
Continue to cook for about 15 minutes. Remove the toothpicks
and serve immediately.

MEDIUM

PETTI DI POLLO CON CAPPERI E LIMONE
Chicken with Capers and Lemon

An old standby, this is one of the easiest and most frequently used recipes I have. It is quite simple to make and very appetizing.

2   whole chicken breasts, boned
     salt and pepper
½   cup flour
¼   cup olive oil
1   garlic clove, minced
4   tablespoons lemon juice
1   teaspoon sage, freshly chopped
½   cup white wine
1   tablespoon capers

Wash and pat the chicken dry. Cut each whole breast in half. Place each breast between waxed paper and pound so that the breast is flat. Season with salt and pepper. Then pat both sides of the chicken with flour.

In a large pan, heat the olive oil and add the chicken breasts. Cook the chicken over medium heat for 3 minutes. Then turn it over and cook for 3 more minutes. Add the chopped garlic clove, lemon juice and chopped sage. Turn the heat to low and continue to sauté for 5 minutes. Add the wine and capers and continue to cook over low heat for 15 minutes.

Place the chicken on a serving platter and pour the remaining caper sauce over the chicken slices.

EASY

Roasted meats are common in the Tuscany region. In many restaurants, you will find a variety of roasted meats, from beef, pork and poultry to game and even wild boar.

VARIATION

Roasted potatoes and carrots also can be prepared in the same pan as the chicken. Arrange the chicken in the middle of a large platter, and place the roasted potatoes all around the edge.

POLLO ARROSTO
Roasted Chicken with Herbs

1	4-pound whole chicken (I find that "free range" chickens are the best; check to see if your butcher carries them)
1	tablespoon butter
3	sage sprigs
3	garlic cloves
	salt and pepper
¼	cup olive oil
½	cup white wine

Wash the chicken inside and out and dry it thoroughly. Place the butter, sage sprigs and peeled garlic inside the chicken cavity. Sprinkle the chicken inside and out with salt and pepper. Tie the legs of the chicken with a string so that the herbs stay inside, flavoring the entire chicken.

Pour the olive oil into a large roasting pan and place the chicken in the pan. Place the pan on a medium rack in an oven preheated to 375 degrees. When the chicken begins to brown, pour on half of the white wine. Turn the chicken over halfway through the cooking time and pour the remaining wine over the browned chicken. Roast for about 1 hour and 45 minutes at 375 degrees.

Cut the chicken into about 10 pieces. Discard the sage and garlic cloves.

EASY

PETTO DI TACCHINO FARCITO
Stuffed Turkey Breast

1	3-pound turkey breast, boned	¼	cup brandy
	salt and pepper	½	cup white wine
3	fresh sage leaves, chopped	½	pound mushrooms
8	slices of prosciutto, thinly sliced	1	garlic clove, minced
1	fresh rosemary sprig, chopped	1	tablespoon parsley,
¼	cup olive oil plus 3 tablespoons		freshly chopped

If possible, ask the butcher to butterfly the turkey breast and to pound it. You should end up with a very large, flat turkey breast.

Lay the turkey breast flat and sprinkle it with salt and pepper. Chop the sage leaves and sprinkle them on the turkey breast. The prosciutto slices should be placed to cover the inside of the turkey breast. The turkey should then be rolled. (The easiest way is to fold in both sides and then to roll.) When completed, tie with a string so that the roll is secured. Tuck fresh rosemary sprigs between the string and the turkey.

In a bowl, combine all the following ingredients: the olive oil, brandy, wine, remaining sage and rosemary. Mix well and use to marinate the turkey breast for about 2 hours.

Wash, scrub and thinly slice the mushrooms. In a medium pan, heat 3 tablespoons of the olive oil, add the mushrooms and mix well. Add the minced garlic clove, chopped parsley and white wine and simmer over low heat for 15 minutes. Put aside.

Preheat the oven to 375 degrees, place the turkey in a roasting pan with the remaining olive oil and ¼ of the marinade and cook for approximately 1 hour and 30 minutes, basting with the marinade as the turkey roll cooks.

After the turkey roll is cooked, remove the string from the roll. Slice the turkey into thick slices, pour the sauce over the turkey and place the mushrooms on top.

> Stuffed meats are fun to make, and they make a great impression on your guests when sliced and placed on a serving platter.

 MEDIUM

POLLO FARCITO CON OLIVE E FUNGHI
Chicken Breasts Stuffed with Olives and Mushrooms

3	whole chicken breasts, boned (6 halves)	½	cup black olives, chopped
¼	pound mushrooms		salt and pepper
3	tablespoons olive oil plus ⅓ cup		flour
1	teaspoon parsley, chopped	4	tablespoons butter
1	garlic clove, minced	1	cup milk
½	cup white wine		

Lay each chicken half between 2 pieces of waxed paper and pound it until it is thin. Wash and slice the mushrooms. Heat 2 tablespoons of the olive oil in a pot and add the sliced mushrooms, cooking over medium heat for about 5 minutes. Add the chopped parsley and garlic and mix. Add the white wine and continue to cook over low heat for about 10 minutes. Then set aside.

Mix 1 tablespoon of the olive oil with the chopped olives. Using a fork, mash the olives into a paste. Set aside.

Lay the chicken breasts flat, sprinkle them with salt and pepper and then spread a teaspoon of the olives and a teaspoon of the sautéed mushrooms. Carefully roll each breast and then tie with a string. Dust each chicken roll lightly with flour.

Heat the remaining olive oil and butter in a large skillet. When the butter foams, add the rolled chicken breast and cook until lightly golden brown (about 3 minutes on each side).

The delicate sauce flavored by the olives and mushrooms will leave your guests with a meal they will never forget.

 MEDIUM

Deglaze the pan with the wine. Add a little salt, cover and cook over low heat for about 30 minutes, gradually adding the milk as the chicken cooks.

Remove the string from each chicken roll and slice each roll into 3 slices. Place the chicken on a platter and pour a generous amount of the sauce over the chicken.

When tying the chicken rolls, don't get discouraged if some of the mixture comes out. Just add the mixture to the sauce while the chicken is cooking.

POLLO AI PEPERONI
Chicken with Bell Peppers

2   chicken breasts, boned (4 halves)
1   green bell pepper
1   red bell pepper
1   yellow bell pepper
1   medium red onion, chopped
⅓   cup olive oil
1   teaspoon sage, chopped
1   teaspoon rosemary, chopped
¼   cup brandy
¾   cup white wine
    salt and pepper

Wash, dry and cut the chicken breasts into 1-by-3-inch pieces.
Wash and seed the bell peppers. Slice the bell peppers into strips
about ½ inch wide. The onion should be sliced into large pieces.

Pour the olive oil into a skillet, add the chicken and turn the heat
on medium high to allow the chicken to brown on both sides.
Add the chopped sage and rosemary. Then pour the brandy over
the chicken, cover and cook for 2 minutes.

Add the onion, sliced bell peppers, white wine, salt and pepper
and allow the mixture to cook for 15 minutes or until the bell
peppers are tender and most of the liquid has evaporated. Transfer
to a serving platter and serve immediately.

This very simple chicken dish
is full of bright flavors
and is a colorful addition
to any meal.

ROTOLO DI TACCHINO ALLA VERDURA
Turkey Breast Stuffed with Spinach

1	pound fresh spinach	1	tablespoon sage, chopped
¼	cup olive oil, plus 1 tablespoon	8	thin slices prosciutto
2	garlic cloves, minced	½	cup dry white wine
3	pounds turkey breast		
	salt and pepper		

Ask your butcher to bone and butterfly the turkey breast and to pound it. You should end up with a very large, flat turkey breast.

Wash and cook the spinach in plenty of water until tender. When the spinach is cooked, drain well and squeeze out any excess water. Finely chop the spinach.

In a medium pan, heat 1 tablespoon of the olive oil, add the minced garlic and sauté for 2 minutes over low heat. Add the chopped spinach and continue to cook for 5 more minutes over low heat. Place the sautéed spinach in a food processor and puree. Set aside.

Rolled meats are very popular in Italy, and there are many versions of them.

Lay out the flattened turkey breast, sprinkle with the salt, pepper and chopped sage. Place the prosciutto slices so as to cover the turkey breast, and place the pureed spinach evenly over the prosciutto. Carefully roll up the meat, enclosing the mixture, and tie it securely with a string.

Preheat the oven to 375 degrees. In a large ovenproof pan, add the olive oil and place the turkey in the pan, cooking at 375 degrees for 1 hour and 30 minutes, occasionally basting with the wine.

When the turkey is cooked, remove the string. Slice the turkey and arrange it on a serving platter. Pour the remaining juices over the turkey slices.

DIFFICULT

POLPETTE SAPORITE
Baked Chicken Croquettes

½ cup olive oil plus 2 tablespoons
2 whole chicken breasts, boned
4 fresh sage leaves
  salt and pepper
¼ cup brandy
2 slices Italian bread
¼ cup chicken broth
3 eggs
2 medium-boiled potatoes
1 tablespoon Parmesan cheese
2 tablespoons parsley, freshly chopped
3 garlic cloves, minced
1 teaspoon thyme
1 cup bread crumbs

In a medium-sized pan, heat 2 tablespoons of the olive oil and add the chicken breast, sage, salt and pepper. Cook until browned on both sides. Add the brandy and continue to cook for 7 more minutes. Remove from the heat and retain the sauce in which the chicken was cooked. Place the chicken in a food processor and chop finely.

Soak the bread slices in the chicken broth. Squeeze the bread to remove excess liquid.

In a large bowl, thoroughly mix the chicken, eggs, potatoes, cheese, parsley, sage, garlic, thyme and bread. Shape the mixture into small balls about the size of a walnut. Coat with the bread crumbs.

Preheat a large ovenproof pan with the remaining olive oil, place the polpette in the pan and bake at 375 degrees for 20 minutes. Turn the polpette and cook for 20 more minutes or until golden brown on both sides.

If you have any leftover roasted chicken or beef, use it instead of the chicken breast to give the croquettes an even better flavor.

VARIATION
The polpette also can be deep fried until golden brown.

 MEDIUM

This is an economical and very popular home-cooked dish. Polpettone is stylish and elegant when served with red bell pepper sauce and roasted potatoes.

POLPETTONE DI TACCHINO ALLA CREMA DI PEPERONE ROSSO
Baked Turkey Loaf with Red Bell Pepper Sauce

1	cup red bell pepper sauce (see page 153 for recipe)
1½	pounds ground turkey
1	cup bread crumbs
¼	cup tomato sauce
2	garlic cloves, minced
1	teaspoon thyme
2	teaspoons parsley, freshly chopped
3	teaspoons sage, freshly chopped
1	tablespoon Parmesan cheese
	salt and pepper
3	eggs
⅓	cup olive oil

Prepare the red bell pepper sauce.

Preheat the oven to 375 degrees.

Thoroughly mix the meat, ½ cup of bread crumbs, tomato sauce, herbs, eggs, cheese, salt and pepper. Shape the meat into a loaf. Coat it with the bread crumbs and bake it in an ovenproof pan coated with the olive oil for 1 hour at 375 degrees.

When the turkey loaf is cooked, slice the loaf and arrange the slices on a serving platter. Add 1 tablespoon of the red bell pepper sauce to each slice.

PESCE AL FORNO CON PATATE
Baked Halibut with Potatoes

3   garlic cloves, minced
1   cup Italian parsley, freshly chopped
¾   cup white wine
2   whole lemons
¼   cup olive oil
    salt and pepper
4   6-ounce halibut steaks
4   medium potatoes, peeled

Finely chop the garlic and parsley, and add the wine, juice of 1 lemon, olive oil, salt and pepper. Use to marinate the halibut steaks for approximately 4 to 6 hours.

Place the halibut steaks and about ¼ cup of the marinade in an ovenproof pan. (The remainder of the marinade will be used as the fish and potatoes are cooking.) Thinly slice the potatoes and layer them on top of the fish. Bake for 10 minutes at 400 degrees. Then pour ¼ cup of the marinade over the potatoes. Lower the heat to 375 degrees and continue to bake for approximately 20 more minutes or until the potatoes are tender.

Garnish with fresh lemon wedges.

This is a popular dish in many of the restaurants in Viareggio.

VARIATION
Other firm fish, such as sea bass or lingcod, can be used in place of halibut.

In Viareggio there is an abundance of fresh fish. I enjoy going to the dock in Viareggio early in the morning and waiting for the fishermen to come in with their fresh catch.

SOGLIOLA AL VINO BIANCO E CAPPERI
Sole with Wine and Caper Sauce

1   tablespoon olive oil
3   tablespoons butter
1   garlic clove, minced
2   tablespoons parsley, chopped
4   medium slices of sole
1   teaspoon lemon rind, minced
¼   cup white wine
1   tablespoon capers
1   lemon

In a large skillet, heat the olive oil and butter until melted. Finely chop the garlic and parsley, add them to the butter and oil and gently sauté over very low heat for 2 or 3 minutes.

Add the fish and the minced lemon rind to the sauce and cook for 2 minutes on each side. Add the white wine and capers to the sauce and continue to cook for approximately 4 more minutes.

Garnish with lemon wedges and serve immediately.

VARIATION

To add a little extra touch, sauté 4 large prawns in a little olive oil. Place 1 prawn on each slice of sole before serving and sprinkle with some freshly chopped parsley.

CACCIUCCO
Fish Stew

3	crabs	1	teaspoon red hot chili pepper, finely chopped
12	mussels	2	lemons, sliced
12	clams	3	medium cans peeled tomatoes
1	pound large prawns	6	cups chicken broth
2	medium yellow onions, finely chopped	2	cups red wine
1	cup olive oil	2	pounds halibut fillet
1	cup Italian parsley, freshly chopped	1	pound red snapper fillet
5	garlic cloves, minced	1	pound sea bass
3	teaspoons salt	12	slices Italian bread
2	teaspoons pepper		

Clean all the shellfish. The crab should be cleaned, broken into smaller pieces and cracked. Clams and mussels should be washed and scrubbed. Devein the prawns, leaving the shell on.

In a large pot, sauté the chopped onion in 1 cup of olive oil for 8 to 10 minutes. Then add the parsley and chopped garlic. Allow the vegetables to simmer on low heat for approximately 10 minutes.

Add all the shellfish and mix well with the olive oil and herbs. Add the salt, pepper, chopped red hot chili pepper, sliced lemons, tomatoes, broth and red wine until the fish is covered by liquid.

Allow to cook on medium to low heat for approximately 45 minutes, stirring occasionally. Add all the other fish and continue to cook on low heat for 25 minutes.

Toast the bread. Rub the garlic on both sides of the toasted bread.

In a large platter, arrange the toasted garlic bread and pour the fish and juices over it. Serve immediately.

This recipe serves about 8 people.

 MEDIUM

SPIEDINI DI PESCE MISTO
Grilled Fish Skewers

½ pound medium prawns
½ pound halibut fillet
½ pound red snapper
½ pound sea bass
½ pound salmon fillet
¼ cup Italian parsley, chopped
2 tablespoons basil, freshly chopped
3 garlic cloves, minced
1 cup dry white wine
   salt and pepper
1 lemon, juice only
⅓ cup olive oil

Clean and devein the prawns, leaving the tails. Wash all the other fish and pat dry. Finely chop the parsley and basil. Mince the garlic.

In a large bowl, combine the wine, olive oil, lemon juice, chopped basil, parsley, garlic, salt and pepper and mix well.

Cut all the fish (other than the prawns) into pieces about 2 inches square. Add all the fish to the marinade and refrigerate for approximately 4 hours.

Arrange 5 to 6 pieces of fish, alternating varieties, on skewers. When the grill is hot, brush it gently with the olive oil. Add the skewers and gently turn every few minutes so that they will not stick to the grill. Brush the fish skewers with the remaining marinade until cooked. Let cook approximately 4 minutes on each side. Serve hot.

These fish skewers can be made either on the barbecue or in the oven broiler.

FRITTO MISTO DI PESCE
Lightly Fried Fish

10   small smelt
½   pound calamari
1   pound medium prawns
    light olive oil
    flour
    salt
2   lemons

Wash and scale the smelt, leaving them whole (although you may remove the heads if you desire). Clean the calamari, and remove the bone, skin and ink sac. Cut the calamari into 1-inch rings, leaving the tentacles whole. Devein the prawns, leaving the shell on.

In a large frying pan, heat the olive oil. Dip the smelt, prawns and calamari in flour. When the oil is hot, fry the fish until golden brown on each side. Drain well on paper towels and sprinkle with salt. Cut the lemons into wedges and serve immediately.

One of my favorite summertime meals in Viareggio is a dish of lightly fried fish and a mixed salad. Most restaurants along the beach in Viareggio offer this dish on their menu. A classic meal is fresh-squeezed lemon over the fish, a mixed salad and a glass of chilled pinot grigio—perfect for dinner at the beach or just a lazy summer day.

TROTE FRITTE
Pan-Fried Trout

6 medium trout
6 rosemary sprigs
3 garlic cloves
  salt
3 tablespoons butter
¼ cup olive oil
¾ cup flour
1 lemon

Clean and gut the trout, removing the head. Pat dry. Wash the rosemary, leaving the sprigs whole. Peel the garlic and cut 3 cloves in half. Place 1 sprig of rosemary and the garlic inside the trout, sprinkle with salt and insert a toothpick to hold the trout together.

In a large frying pan, heat the butter and olive oil. Dip the trout into the flour and place it into the pan. Allow the fish to brown on each side for about 3 minutes. When the trout is cooked, remove the toothpick, rosemary sprig and garlic. Serve on a platter with lemon wedges.

VARIATION
To cook the trout in the oven: Preheat the oven to 350 degrees. In a cast-iron or other heavy ovenproof pan, add the butter and 3 tablespoons of olive oil and heat in the oven until the butter has melted. Flour the trout on both sides, place it into the pan and cook for 5 minutes on each side.

FILETTI DI SALMONE CON SALSA DI YOGURT
Broiled Salmon Fillets with Yogurt Sauce

This is a rather unusual sauce, with the yogurt adding a slightly tart note. However, you will find it an elegant complement to the salmon.

4   6-ounce salmon fillets
1   tablespoon olive oil
¼   cup onion, chopped
2   fresh rosemary sprigs
¼   cup light cream
1   teaspoon butter
¾   cup plain yogurt
    fresh chives

Brush the salmon fillets with olive oil and broil them for approximately 4 minutes on each side. Sauté the chopped onion and rosemary sprigs in the butter for 5 minutes. Add the cream and yogurt. Then simmer over low heat for 5 minutes. Add salt and simmer for 5 more minutes. Remove the rosemary sprigs.

Arrange the broiled salmon fillets on a serving dish. Spoon the sauce over each fillet and add the chives as garnish.

MEDIUM

Your guests will think you
worked for hours to put this
recipe together. It looks great
and tastes wonderful. Serve with
boiled red potatoes and
asparagus with lemon and
parsley sauce.

FILETTI DI SOGLIOLA ALLA SENAPE
Sole with Mustard Sauce

8	large prawns
2	tablespoons olive oil
1	teaspoon parsley, chopped
1	garlic clove, minced
	salt
½	cup white wine
1	tablespoon lemon juice
	flour
8	medium fillets of sole
4	tablespoons butter
1	tablespoon dijon mustard

Peel, devein and coarsely chop the prawns. In a small pan, heat
1 tablespoon of the olive oil, add the prawns, chopped parsley
and minced garlic and sprinkle with salt. Cook for 2 minutes on
medium heat. Add 2 tablespoons of the wine, lemon juice and
1 teaspoon of flour. Cook for 2 more minutes, stirring constantly.
Then set aside.

Lay the fillets flat and place a tablespoon of the prawn mixture on
each one. Roll the fillets, seal them with the toothpicks and then
dip them in the flour.

In a baking dish, add the butter, remaining olive oil and mustard
and place in a preheated oven at 325 degrees for 5 minutes.
When the butter has melted, add the fillets. Bake at 350 degrees
for about 5 minutes, pour in the remainder of the wine, turn the
fillets over, baste them with the sauce and continue to cook them
for 5 more minutes.

Remove the toothpicks, arrange the fillets on a serving dish and
spoon the sauce over each one.

MEDIUM

GAMBERETTI SALTATI
Sautéed Prawns

3 medium-ripe tomatoes
1 pound medium prawns
¼ cup olive oil
2 garlic cloves, minced
3 tablespoons parsley, chopped
½ cup dry white wine
½ teaspoon salt

Peel, seed and finely chop the tomatoes. Wash and devein the prawns, but do not remove the shells. Heat the olive oil, add the chopped garlic and sauté for 2 minutes over low heat. Add the chopped tomatoes and parsley and continue to sauté for 5 minutes. Next, add the prawns, white wine and salt and cook uncovered over medium heat for 8 minutes, stirring occasionally.

Remove from the heat and serve immediately.

Cooking prawns this way emphasizes their natural sweetness. The tomatoes may be left out of this recipe.

TRANCI DI TONNO IN PADELLA
Fresh Tuna Steaks

3 garlic cloves, minced
2 fresh rosemary sprigs, chopped
¾ cup dry white wine
   salt and pepper
4 8-ounce tuna steaks
¼ cup virgin olive oil plus 2 tablespoons
2 tablespoons capers
1 lemon, juice only

Mince the garlic and chop the rosemary. In a large bowl, combine
the wine, salt, pepper, garlic and rosemary. Add the tuna steaks
and marinate them for at least 2 hours, turning occasionally.

In a small bowl, add the olive oil, lemon juice and capers.
Whisk well. Set the caper sauce aside.

Heat 2 tablespoons of olive oil in a cast-iron pan. Add the tuna
steaks for 3 to 4 minutes on each side, basting with the marinade
while cooking. Remove the tuna steaks. Place them on a serving
platter and drizzle with the caper sauce.

PESCE BOLLITO AL VINO BIANCO
Poached Halibut in White Wine

1½ cups dry white wine
3 whole garlic cloves
2 fresh rosemary sprigs
1½ lemons
2 pounds halibut fillet
3 tablespoons virgin olive oil
  pinch of salt

In a medium pot, combine the white wine, garlic cloves and rosemary sprigs. Squeeze the juice from ½ of the lemon and put the remaining ½ of the lemon into the pot. Add 1 tablespoon of olive oil and the fish.

Bring the liquid to a boil. Then lower the heat and simmer gently for 10 minutes. Remove the fish from the heat and allow it to stand for 5 minutes. Drain the fish and transfer it to a serving dish. Drizzle with the remaining olive oil and squeeze the remainder of the lemon juice over the top.

When the halibut is fresh, this is truly an exquisite dish. The virgin olive oil gives an elegant flavor to this fish.

VARIATION
If halibut is unavailable, other firm white fish can be substituted, such as salmon, sea bass or lingcod.

The beautiful simplicity of this recipe is that the fish simply cooks in its own juices and retains the wonderful flavor of fresh sea bass.

BRANZINO AL CARTOCCIO
Baked Sea Bass

1¾ pounds sea bass
     pinch of salt
2 tablespoons Italian parsley, chopped
¼ cup olive oil
1 lemon, juice only
1 garlic clove, minced

Place the fish on aluminum foil and season with the salt, parsley and garlic. Add the olive oil and lemon juice. Fold the edges of the aluminum foil to enclose the fish completely.

Preheat the oven to 400 degrees and bake for 20 minutes.

Remove the fish from the foil and serve with fresh lemon juice.

GAMBERI IN GUAZZETTO
Prawns in White Wine

1   pound large prawns
⅓   cup olive oil
1   tablespoon parsley, chopped
2   garlic cloves, minced
¾   cup dry white wine
1   teaspoon lemon rind, grated
    pinch of salt

Wash and devein the prawns, leaving the shells on. Heat the olive oil in a large skillet, add the prawns and cook over medium heat for 2 minutes on each side, turning the prawns only once.

Add the chopped parsley, minced garlic, white wine, lemon and salt and continue to sauté over low heat for 8 minutes.

What a simple, yet wonderful way to serve prawns! In Italy, the simplest way of preparing fish usually is preferred.

BACCALÀ
Dried Cod in Tomato Sauce

1½	pounds dried cod
½	cup olive oil
1	15-ounce can peeled tomatoes
1	large onion, chopped
3	garlic cloves, minced
1	celery stalk, chopped
½	cup Italian parsley, chopped
	pinch of pepper
½	cup chicken broth

Soak the cod for at least 24 hours in the water, changing the water occasionally. Drain well and cut the cod into 3-inch-square pieces. In a large skillet, heat the olive oil and gently fry the cod for 8 minutes over low heat. Remove the cod with a slotted spoon and put it aside.

Chop the tomatoes finely and set them aside. Finely chop the onion, garlic and celery stalk. In the same skillet in which the cod was fried, add the chopped vegetables and parsley and sauté over low heat for 5 minutes. Add the chopped tomatoes and pepper, continue to cook for 5 minutes and then add the fried cod and broth to the skillet. Cover and then simmer over low heat for 1 hour. Stir occasionally.

 MEDIUM

VERDURE VEGETABLES

Tuscany is one of the richest areas for growing vegetables in all of Italy. This is one of the reasons why vegetables are so prominently featured in many Northern Italian dishes. Even homes with small gardens produce fresh vegetables and herbs. The countryside of Lucca is filled with fresh greens, tomatoes and zucchini growing in abundance. For those who have no room to garden, the local *fruttivendolo* (green grocer) has a wide variety of vegetables available. All herbs also can be found at the local vegetable market. *Un mazzetto di odori,* meaning "a bouquet of herbs," is sold in the vegetable market and is comprised of celery, carrot, parsley and sometimes basil.

The sweetest peas usually are picked in the springtime in Tuscany, when they are especially tender.

CARCIOFI E PISELLI
Peas and Artichokes

10 baby artichokes
½ lemon
¼ cup olive oil
1 small yellow onion, chopped
1 garlic clove, minced
¼ cup tomato sauce
   salt and pepper
2 cups fresh peas or 1 sixteen-ounce package of frozen peas
¾ cup chicken broth
1 teaspoon mint, chopped

Clean and remove the tough outer leaves of the artichokes. Cut the artichokes in half and place them in the water with the lemon half to prevent them from turning brown.

In a medium-sized saucepan, add the olive oil, chopped onion and garlic and sauté for approximately 5 minutes. Add the sliced artichokes and sauté over low heat for 5 minutes. Next, add the chopped mint, tomato sauce, salt and pepper and simmer on low heat, covered, for about 10 minutes or until the artichokes are tender. Add the peas and ¾ cup of chicken broth, continuing to cook over low heat for 15 minutes or until most of the liquid has evaporated.

Place in a serving dish and garnish with fresh mint leaves.

 MEDIUM

FUNGHI E ZUCCHINE
Mushrooms and Zucchini

1 pound fresh mushrooms
5 small to medium zucchini
½ medium yellow onion, chopped
2 garlic cloves, minced
½ cup Italian parsley, chopped
⅓ cup olive oil
  salt and pepper
2 tablespoons white wine

Clean and thickly slice the mushrooms. Wash the zucchini and cut them into 1-inch wedges. Finely chop the onion, garlic and parsley. In a large saucepan, heat the olive oil and sauté the zucchini and mushrooms over low heat for approximately 5 minutes. Add the onion, garlic, parsley, salt and pepper and cook over very low heat for an additional 5 minutes. Finally, add the white wine and continue to cook for 15 minutes and serve.

The marriage of mushrooms and zucchini gives this vegetable dish a delicious and intense flavor.

PATATE AL POMODORO
Potatoes with Fresh Tomatoes

This is a popular Tuscan way of informally preparing potatoes.

½ cup olive oil
4 medium russet potatoes
2 medium-ripe red tomatoes
2 garlic cloves, minced
1 fresh sage sprig
  salt and pepper
1 teaspoon parsley, chopped

Heat the olive oil in a large skillet. Cut the potatoes into 1-inch cubes. When the oil is hot, add the potatoes and cook over medium heat for approximately 15 minutes or until they are golden brown. Wash the tomatoes, peel them and chop them coarsely. Mince the garlic. Set aside.

When the potatoes are almost cooked, add the tomatoes, sage sprig, salt, pepper and minced garlic. Mix well and continue to cook over low heat for approximately 15 minutes. Sprinkle with the chopped parsley.

CAROTE AL MARSALA
Carrots with Marsala

1 pound carrots
5 tablespoons butter
¾ cup marsala wine
1 teaspoon salt
1 tablespoon parsley, chopped

Peel, wash and dry the carrots. Slice the carrots diagonally, approximately ⅛ inch thick. In a large skillet, heat the butter until it foams, add the carrots and sauté over medium heat for approximately 10 minutes. Add marsala wine and salt and continue to cook over medium heat for about 5 minutes. Lower the heat and cover, continuing to cook for 15 minutes or until desired tenderness.

Place in a serving dish and pour the remaining liquid over the carrots. Garnish with chopped parsley.

Marsala is a wine that is either fragrant and sweet or dry. It is used in poultry, vegetable and meat dishes.

Fresh greens cover the hillsides of Lucca. In the small towns outside of Lucca, you can see the women out early in the morning, picking greens to prepare for the day's lunch or dinner.

VERDURA SFRITTA
Simple Greens

2 pounds fresh greens
   (for instance, spinach, mustard, swiss chard)
½ cup olive oil
3 garlic cloves, minced
   salt

Wash and rinse all the greens. In a large pot, bring water to a boil and add the cleaned greens. Allow the greens to cook for about 15 minutes or until tender.

Drain the greens well and squeeze out all the excess water. Chop finely.

In a large pan, heat the olive oil, add the minced garlic and sauté over low heat until the oil is flavored. Add the chopped greens, salt as desired and sauté for approximately 10 minutes over low heat.

PATATE ARROSTO CON SALVIA
E ROSMARINO
Roasted Potatoes with Sage and Rosemary

These are best served with roast
beef or roasted chicken.

20   small red potatoes
20   fresh sage leaves
10   fresh rosemary sprigs, chopped
¼   cup olive oil
        salt and pepper

Scrub and wash the potatoes and dry them well. Make a slit in
each potato halfway through. Insert 1 sage leaf and a small pinch
of chopped rosemary.

Place the olive oil in the roasting pan and sit the potatoes upright,
with the slits facing upward. Lightly season with salt and pepper.
Place the pan in an oven preheated to 375 degrees for 55 minutes.
Gently turn the potatoes once to brown each side.

Green beans in Italy typically are picked when they are small and very tender. However, when preparing these green beans Italian style, choose the most mature green beans possible and fresh, vine-ripened tomatoes.

FAGIOLINI IN UMIDO
Green Beans in Tomato Sauce

1   pound fresh green beans
½   cup olive oil
2   medium-ripe tomatoes
3   garlic cloves, minced
     salt and pepper

Wash the green beans and cut them in half. Bring the water to a boil, add the beans and cook them until they are tender. Do not overcook. Drain well.

Heat the olive oil in a large saucepan. Add the peeled, seeded and chopped tomatoes and sauté over low heat for 5 minutes. Add the chopped garlic, salt and pepper as desired and continue to cook for approximately 10 minutes over low heat. Then add the green beans, continuing to cook over low heat for 15 more minutes, mix well and serve.

FRITTO MISTO DI VERDURE
Mixed Fried Vegetables

6 small artichokes
2 medium zucchini
1 green tomato
3 large mushrooms
2 eggs
1 cup flour
2 tablespoons milk
1 cup light olive oil
    salt as desired
1 lemon, cut into 6 wedges

Wash all the vegetables and dry them well. Remove all the tough outer leaves on the artichokes. Slice the zucchini lengthwise into about 4 slices. Cut the artichokes in half. Slice the green tomato and mushrooms into ⅛-inch slices.

Beat the eggs with a fork, add flour and blend well. Add the milk and salt and beat again.

Heat the olive oil in a large, deep skillet. Place the sliced zucchini in the batter and coat them well. Deep-fry until they are golden brown on both sides. Repeat this process with the other vegetables. Serve immediately.

Serve on a platter with lemon wedges.

 MEDIUM

In Italy, fresh lemon is always served with fried foods because, they say, lemon juice enhances the flavor of the fried food.

VARIATION
Other vegetables, such as cauliflower and asparagus, also can be used.

These beans are also excellent when served cold.

FAGIOLINI, AGLIO, OLIO E PREZZEMOLO
Green Beans with Garlic, Parsley and Olive Oil

½   cup Italian parsley, chopped
3   garlic cloves, minced
1   pound green beans
½   cup olive oil
½   lemon, juice only
    salt

Chop the parsley and garlic finely. Wash the green beans and cut them in half. Bring a pot of water to a boil, add the green beans and cook them until they are tender. Drain them well and place them in a bowl. Add the olive oil, parsley, garlic, lemon juice and salt. Toss the green beans to mix well.

PATATE AL LATTE
Potatoes with Milk

6 medium potatoes
1 garlic clove, minced
½ cup parsley, freshly chopped
4 tablespoons butter
salt and pepper
⅛ teaspoon nutmeg
1¼ cups milk

Peel, wash and dry the potatoes. Cube the potatoes into 1-inch pieces and set them aside. Chop the garlic and parsley finely.

In a large pan, heat the butter over medium heat and add the cubed potatoes. Sprinkle with salt, pepper and grated nutmeg, mix well and add the milk. Allow to cook over low heat for approximately 30 minutes, stirring frequently. Sprinkle parsley and garlic over the potatoes.

The potatoes are cooked when most of the liquid has evaporated.

Potatoes are a popular vegetable in Tuscany. This potato recipe is also wonderful when topped with sautéed porcini mushrooms.

Aprile temperato,
buon per quel contadin
che ha seminato.
(Fair weather in April, good for the farmer who sowed.)

Leftover peperonata makes a tasty lunch the next day. Heat leftover peperonata in a small skillet, add 2 eggs and cook to desired taste.

PEPERONATA
Green, Red and Yellow Bell Peppers in Tomato Sauce

1   medium onion, chopped
2   green bell peppers, seeded
2   red bell peppers, seeded
2   yellow bell peppers, seeded
⅓   cup olive oil
3   medium-ripe tomatoes
2   tablespoons tomato sauce
    salt and pepper
¼   cup chicken broth

Chop the onion coarsely. Wash, seed and slice the peppers into 2-inch strips.

In a large pan, heat the olive oil, add the onions and sauté over medium heat for 3 minutes. Add the bell peppers and cook them over low heat until the peppers are tender. Chop the tomatoes coarsely and add them to the bell peppers. Add the tomato sauce, salt and pepper, cover and cook over medium heat for 10 minutes. Add the broth and cook uncovered for an additional 5 minutes. Remove from heat and serve.

MEDIUM

FAGIOLI ALL'UCCELLETTO
Beans in Sauce

This bean dish is very typical of the Tuscan region and is often served with a mild sausage.

1   pound dried cannellini or dried cranberry beans
2   fresh rosemary sprigs
3   garlic cloves, minced
1   teaspoon salt
½   cup olive oil
½   cup tomato sauce
1   medium tomato
4   fresh sage sprigs
1   teaspoon pepper
1   cup light broth

Soak the beans in water overnight. Boil the beans in plenty of water for about 45 minutes, adding 2 sprigs of rosemary, one garlic clove, and a teaspoon of salt. When the beans are cooked, drain well.

In a large skillet, heat the olive oil, add the garlic and sauté over low heat for about 3 minutes. Add the tomato sauce and chopped tomato and allow to simmer for about 10 minutes over low heat. Add the beans, sage, salt and pepper.

Continue to cook over low heat for about 10 minutes. Add ½ cup of the broth and simmer until the beans have absorbed most of the liquid.

For a quick and easy meal, grill a steak and spread 2 tablespoons of mushrooms over the meat.

FUNGHI AL VINO BIANCO
Mushrooms in White Wine

1 pound mushrooms
¼ cup olive oil
1 tablespoon butter
1 tablespoon lemon juice
2 garlic cloves, minced
¼ cup parsley, freshly chopped
  salt and pepper
¼ cup white wine

Wash and slice the mushrooms. Heat the olive oil and butter in a pan. Add the sliced mushrooms and lemon juice and cook over medium heat for about 5 minutes. Add the minced garlic, parsley, salt and pepper and stir. Finally, add the wine. Continue to cook over low heat for 10 minutes or until the mushrooms are tender.

ASPARAGI AL LIMONE E PREZZEMOLO
Asparagus with Lemon and Parsley

1   pound fresh asparagus
½   cup parsley, freshly chopped
⅓   cup lemon juice
3   tablespoons olive oil
     salt and pepper

Wash the asparagus and trim off the tougher part of the asparagus stalk. Steam the asparagus until it reaches the desired tenderness.

Chop the parsley finely. Combine the parsley, lemon juice, olive oil, salt and pepper in a bowl and whisk well. Pour the mixture over the asparagus and serve.

This vegetable dish is best prepared when the asparagus is young and tender.

A popular way of serving a variety of vegetables. Celery, fennel or asparagus also can be used in this dish. Remember, the Italians enjoy their vegetables well cooked, until they are no longer crisp.

Trist è quell' anno, che il baco non fa danno.
(Sad is the year that the worm does no damage to the crop.)

VERDURE MISTE IN PADELLA
Mixed Vegetables Sauté

1	potato
2	carrots
1	onion
6	broccoli florets
6	cauliflower florets
8	brussels sprouts
½	cabbage
2	celery stalks
⅓	cup olive oil
	salt
1	cup white wine
½	cup chicken broth

Wash and dry all the vegetables. Slice the carrots and celery diagonally about ⅛ of an inch thick, slice the onion into thick wedges, halve the brussels sprouts, cut the broccoli and cauliflower into florets, slice the cabbage and cube the potatoes into 1-inch pieces.

In a large pan, heat the olive oil and add all the cut vegetables. Stir the vegetables well, add salt and cook for 5 minutes over low heat. Add the white wine and broth to the vegetables. Cover the pan and cook for 10 more minutes. Uncover and allow ½ of the liquid to evaporate (approximately 10 more minutes).

CAVOLFIORE IN BIANCO
Cauliflower in White Sauce

2 cups béchamel sauce
(see page 148 for recipe)
1 large cauliflower
3 tablespoons butter
salt
½ cup Parmesan cheese, freshly grated
½ cup bread crumbs

Prepare the béchamel sauce.

Wash and dry the cauliflower and cut it into florets. Steam until firm but tender. Butter a medium Pyrex baking dish. Place the florets in one layer, sprinkle with salt and add the béchamel sauce and grated Parmesan cheese. Top with the bread crumbs and butter.

Bake for 10 minutes in oven at 375 degrees. Then place under the broiler for 3 minutes or until golden brown.

The first time I went to buy a cauliflower in Lucca, I couldn't find one. Little did I know that I was walking right past them. The cauliflower in Italy is much smaller than what we are accustomed to in America. It is also completely enclosed in its leaves and stalks, which are also tasty.

Fragrant prosciutto gives these stuffed onions an elegant and distinct flavor.

CIPOLLE RIPIENE
Stuffed Onions

8   medium yellow or white onions
½   cup bread crumbs
½   cup milk
1   tablespoon olive oil
4   ounces prosciutto, chopped
⅓   cup Parmesan cheese, grated
      salt and pepper
1   egg
2   tablespoons butter
⅓   cup broth

Skin the onions and cook them for 10 minutes in salted boiling water. Cut the tops and scoop out a small portion of the center of the onion. Place the onions upside down, allowing them to drain and dry.

Soak the bread crumbs in milk for 5 minutes. Then squeeze the bread crumbs to remove excess liquid. In a small pan, heat the olive oil and add the chopped prosciutto. Cook for 3 minutes over low heat. Then remove.

In a large bowl, combine the prosciutto, cheese, bread crumbs, salt, pepper and egg.

Preheat the oven to 375 degrees. Grease a baking dish with butter.

Fill each onion with a generous spoonful of the mixture and arrange in the baking dish. Dot each onion with butter and add the broth and remaining butter to the dish.

Bake for 40 minutes, periodically basting with the juices. Serve hot.

 MEDIUM

ASPARAGI CON PROSCIUTTO
Asparagus with Prosciutto

This is an elegant accompaniment to any meat or poultry dish.

24 asparagus spears
 3 tablespoons butter
 6 thin slices of prosciutto
 1 teaspoon lemon juice
     salt
½ cup bread crumbs
⅓ cup Parmesan cheese, freshly grated

Trim the asparagus spears down to 6 or 7 inches.

Bring a large pot of water to a boil, add the asparagus spears, boil for 2 minutes and drain well.

Butter a baking dish that is large enough to hold the asparagus. Wrap 1 slice of prosciutto around 4 of the asparagus spears and place them in the dish. Repeat until all the asparagus spears have been wrapped with prosciutto. Sprinkle them with lemon juice and salt. Dust the spears with Parmesan cheese and bread crumbs. Dot with the butter.

Bake in an oven at 350 degrees for 10 minutes. Set the pan under the broiler for about 3 minutes. Remove and serve immediately.

Prosciutto is a delicate salt-cured ham. The finest are prosciutto di Parma and prosciutto San Daniele. Prosciutto has a pinkish red color and a delicate aroma.

PISELLI CON PROSCIUTTO
Peas with Prosciutto

1   small red onion, chopped
¼   cup olive oil
¼   pound prosciutto (purchase one ¼-pound slice; then dice)
3   cups fresh peas or 2 sixteen-ounce packages of frozen peas
1   tablespoon parsley, freshly chopped
¼   cup white wine
¼   cup chicken broth
    salt and pepper

Finely chop the red onion. Heat the olive oil in a medium skillet and add the chopped onion. Sauté over low heat for 10 minutes.

Add the diced prosciutto to the pan and cook for 2 minutes. Add the peas and parsley and mix well. Add the white wine, broth, salt and pepper and continue to cook over low heat for 20 more minutes.

MEDIUM

SFORMATO TRI-COLORE
Three-Colored Vegetable Mold

3 cups béchamel sauce (see page 148 for recipe)
1 pound carrots
2 pounds fresh spinach
1 pound cauliflower
¼ cup olive oil

2 garlic cloves, minced
1 teaspoon nutmeg, freshly grated
½ cup Parmesan cheese, grated
salt and pepper
4 eggs

Steam the carrots, spinach and cauliflower separately.

In a skillet, heat the olive oil and minced garlic. Add the chopped spinach and sauté over low heat for 5 minutes.

In a food processor, separately puree the carrots, spinach and cauliflower and place them in individual bowls. Divide the béchamel sauce evenly among the three pureed vegetables. Divide the nutmeg, Parmesan, salt and pepper into three equal parts also. Add 2 eggs to the spinach mixture, 1 egg to the carrots and 1 egg to the cauliflower. Mix each one well.

Butter a 10-inch-diameter ovenproof mold and add the spinach mixture, cauliflower layer and then the carrot mixture.

Place the mold in a larger ovenproof pan and pour about 1½ inches of water into the bottom of the larger pan. Place the vegetable mold inside the larger pan and bake in a preheated oven for 1 hour at 350 degrees.

Allow to stand for 5 minutes before removing from the mold pan. Loosen the vegetable mold by inserting a knife around the edge of the mold. While it is still warm, turn it out onto a serving plate.

DIFFICULT

This is an elegant and delicate vegetable dish.

Potatoes grown in Tuscany are very small and are golden colored on the inside. Similar potatoes grown in the United States include Yukon gold, gold nugget and yellow finn.

PATATE, CAROTE E CIPOLLE ARROSTO
Roasted Potatoes, Carrots and Onions

4 medium potatoes
4 carrots
8 small onions
8 fresh sage leaves, chopped
4 whole garlic cloves
⅔ cup olive oil
  salt and pepper

Peel, rinse and cut the potatoes into 2-inch pieces. Slice the carrots into 3-inch wedges. Remove the skin from the onions. Coarsely chop the sage. Leave the garlic whole with the skin on.

In a large ovenproof skillet, add the olive oil and preheat the oven to 375 degrees. When the skillet is heated, add all the vegetables, chopped sage, whole garlic cloves, salt and pepper.

Cook at 375 degrees for 1 hour, periodically turning the vegetables so they do not stick to the bottom of the pan.

CARDI FRITTI
Fried Cardoon

1½ pounds cardoon
1 lemon
2 eggs
¾ cup flour
3 tablespoons milk
   salt
1½ cups olive oil
½ lemon

Wash the cardoon with cold water. Discard the tough outer stems and remove the strings from the inner stalks. Cut the cardoon in 3- to 4-inch pieces.

Cook the cardoon in a large pot of boiling water, adding the lemon, for 35 to 40 minutes or until tender. Drain and set aside.

Prepare a batter by beating together the eggs, flour, milk and a pinch of salt.

Heat the olive oil in a large frying pan. Dip the cardoon into the batter and deep-fry until golden brown on each side. Drain on paper towels.

Fresh cardoon should be served hot, garnished with fresh lemon wedges.

Cardoon can be boiled and cooked 2 to 3 days in advance, then refrigerated until ready to use.

MEDIUM

Cardoon is a vegetable that grows well in the cold climate of Northern Italy. It resembles the stalks of an artichoke plant and looks like large celery.

SUGHI SAUCES

The recipes included in this section are the building blocks for most Italian recipes.
Northern Italian cooking uses lighter, creamier sauces with delicate flavors.

A white sauce used predominantly in Northern Italy over pasta, vegetables and even fish.

BESCIAMELLA
Béchamel

6 tablespoons butter
3 cups milk
6 tablespoons flour
1 teaspoon salt
⅛ teaspoon nutmeg

Melt the butter in a medium pot. In a separate pot, heat the milk but do not boil it. Add the flour to the melted butter and mix well. Slowly add the heated milk to the butter mixture and mix well until all the milk has been added, stirring constantly over medium heat. Add the salt and freshly grated nutmeg.
Cook until the mixture comes to a boil and has thickened. Then remove from heat.

Makes approximately 2½ cups of béchamel sauce.

MEDIUM

SALSA VERDE
Green Sauce

This sauce is excellent for fish dishes and boiled meats.

½ cup parsley, freshly chopped
1 garlic clove
3 tablespoons capers
4 anchovies
1 slice sourdough bread
2 tablespoons white vinegar
½ lemon, juice only
¼ cup olive oil
1 teaspoon salt

Chop the parsley and garlic finely and set aside. Chop the capers and anchovies coarsely. Remove the crust from the bread, discard the crust and soak the remainder of the bread in vinegar. Squeeze the bread to eliminate the excess vinegar.

In a medium-sized bowl, add all the ingredients, squeeze in the lemon juice and combine well.

This sauce is exceptionally flavorful when prepared with fresh tomatoes. An excellent sauce, it is perfect for pasta or in a risotto dish.

POMAROLA
Basic Tomato Sauce with Herbs

  5 tomatoes
 ½ cup olive oil
  1 small onion, chopped
  1 stalk celery, chopped
  1 carrot, chopped
  2 garlic cloves, minced
 ¼ cup parsley, chopped
 ¼ cup basil, chopped
     salt

Wash, peel and seed the tomatoes and chop coarsely. Wash and dry all the other vegetables.

In a large pot, heat the olive oil, add the tomatoes and simmer over medium heat for 10 minutes. Coarsely chop the carrot, onion, celery and all the other vegetables. Add them to the tomatoes. Add chopped herbs. Add salt and simmer on low heat for 30 minutes. In a food processor, puree the tomato mixture, return it to the pot and continue to cook for 10 minutes.

Pesto I

  2 tablespoons pine nuts
½ cup basil, chopped
  2 garlic cloves
½ cup olive oil
      salt
½ cup Parmesan cheese, freshly grated

Toast the pine nuts in the oven at 350 degrees for 8 minutes, remove them and set them aside.

Wash, dry and finely chop the basil and garlic. In a bowl, combine the olive oil, pine nuts, salt and chopped herbs. Mix and add the Parmesan cheese. The mixture can be made up to 4 days in advance if it is kept refrigerated.

Pesto II

¼ cup basil, chopped
¼ cup Italian parsley, chopped
  4 garlic cloves
½ cup olive oil
¼ cup pecorino cheese, freshly grated
      pinch of salt

In a food processor, add all the ingredients and puree them until the pesto sauce is creamy.

Pesto is best made during the summer months, when basil is in season.

Il miglior condimento e' l'appetito.
(The best condiment is an appetite.)

Sugo di Carne
Meat Sauce

 MEDIUM

1 carrot	1½ pounds beef (1¼-inch-thick cut of beef, such as eye of round)
1 celery stalk	½ cup white wine
1 medium yellow or white onion	2 tomatoes
½ cup parsley, chopped	2 garlic cloves
1 cup olive oil	salt and pepper
1 whole chicken breast, boned and skinned	⅓ cup tomato paste
2 lean pork chops (about 1 inch thick)	1 cup water
	1 cup chicken broth
	4 10-ounce cans tomato sauce

Finely mince the carrot, celery stalk and onion. Chop the parsley and put it aside.

Heat the olive oil in a large pot. Place the chicken breast and pork chops in the pot and brown them well on both sides over medium heat for about 10 minutes. Remove the chicken and pork chops and put in the beef. Cook the beef as long as needed for the type of cut being used (about 10 minutes).

Deglaze the pot with the wine, and use a wooden spoon to scrape the bottom of the pot so that nothing sticks. Add the chopped vegetables and parsley and cook over low heat for 10 minutes.

Remove the bones from the pork chops. In a food processor, chop all the meats and place them in a large bowl.

To this day, the wonderful smell of meat sauce reminds me of Sundays in Gattaiola, a small town outside of Lucca. My friend Diva would get up very early in the morning and prepare this sauce for a special Sunday lunch, usually served over tortelli or gnocchi.

Peel and seed the tomatoes and chop them very finely. Mince the garlic and place it in the pot, mixing well. Add the chopped meats and combine them well with the vegetables. Add salt and pepper as desired. Add the chopped tomatoes and continue to cook over low heat for about 10 minutes. Add the tomato paste diluted in water, broth and tomato sauce.

Cook over low heat for about 1½ hours, stirring occasionally. If the sauce seems too thick, additional chicken broth can be added. When the sauce is cooked, remove it from the heat.

SALSA DI PEPERONE ROSSO
Red Bell Pepper Sauce

2 red bell peppers
½ red onion
¼ cup olive oil plus 1 tablespoon
¼ cup dry white wine
2 tablespoons tomato sauce
½ teaspoon salt

Wash, seed and thinly slice the bell peppers. Coarsely chop the onion.

In a medium pan, heat the olive oil, add the onion and bell peppers and sauté over low heat for 5 minutes. Add the white wine, tomato sauce and salt and continue to cook on low heat for 20 minutes.

In a food processor, puree the red bell pepper sauce. Return it to the pan, drizzle with 1 tablespoon of olive oil and cook for 5 minutes over low heat.

The red bell pepper sauce can be prepared up to 2 days before it is used, as long as it is kept refrigerated.

This sauce is an excellent accompaniment to meat, fish or grilled polenta.

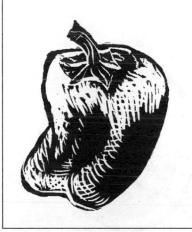

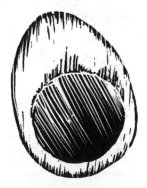

UOVA EGGS

These egg dishes can be meals themselves. Tuscans use eggs in a variety of ways, including in the frittata recipes found here. *Frittata* means "fried" and designates numerous omelette-like dishes loaded with healthy vegetables, light cheeses and meat sauces.

FRITTATA DI SPINACI
Spinach Frittata

Frittata is good when served either hot or cold. I enjoy a slice of leftover frittata in a sandwich. It can be cut into small squares and served also as an appetizer.

1   pound spinach
⅓   cup olive oil
3   garlic cloves, minced
1   teaspoon salt
5   eggs

Bring a pot of water to a boil, add the cleaned spinach and cook until tender. When the spinach is cooked, drain it well and squeeze out all the excess water. Finely chop the spinach.

In a large nonstick pan, add the olive oil and minced garlic. Sauté over low heat for 3 minutes, add the chopped spinach and salt and sauté over low heat for 7 minutes.

Beat the eggs in a large bowl. Add the eggs to the spinach and cook for 5 minutes over low heat. Gently slide the frittata onto a flat plate, place the pan over the dish and turn the frittata upside down. Continue to cook for 7 more minutes or until the frittata is golden brown on each side.

UOVA AL POMODORO
Eggs with Tomato Sauce

A typical Lucchese egg dish, this one is great for lunch or a light dinner.

3 medium tomatoes
⅓ cup olive oil
1 teaspoon parsley, freshly chopped
¼ teaspoon red hot chili pepper, finely chopped (optional)
4 eggs
   salt

Peel and seed the tomatoes and coarsely chop them. Heat the olive oil in a large pan. Add the tomatoes, parsley and chili pepper and cook them over low heat for 5 minutes.

Break the eggs into the skillet and cook them for 2 minutes. Cover the skillet. Reduce the heat and continue to cook for 4 more minutes. Remove from heat and serve.

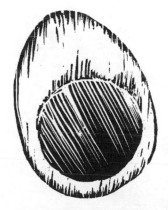

These eggs are absolutely wonderful for breakfast or lunch. The fontina cheese adds a delicious flavor to this dish.

UOVA IN CARROZZA
Eggs in a Cart

4   1-inch slices of Italian bread
1   tablespoon butter
4   eggs
    salt and pepper
4   slices fontina cheese

Cut a 2-inch-square hole in each slice of bread.

Heat the butter over medium heat in a large pan. Place the bread in the pan and allow it to brown for 2 minutes. Break 1 egg in each hole and continue to cook for 1 minute. Gently turn each slice of bread with egg over, sprinkle it with salt and pepper and place 1 slice of the cheese on it. Cook as long as desired.

FRITTATA DI ZUCCHINE
Zucchini Omelet

¼ cup olive oil
6 medium zucchini
  salt and pepper
1 medium onion, chopped
1 tablespoon parsley, chopped
5 eggs

Heat the olive oil in a nonstick pan.

Slice the zucchini thinly, place the pieces on a plate, sprinkle them with salt and allow them to sit for about 20 minutes to remove the excess water.

Chop the onion and add to the heated olive oil. In a bowl, break the eggs, add the chopped parsley, season with salt and pepper, beat with a fork and set aside. Add the drained zucchini to the pan and cook until tender (about 10 minutes). Add the egg mixture to the zucchini and allow to cook for about 5 minutes on one side. Gently slide the frittata onto a flat plate, put the pan over the dish and turn the frittata upside down back into the pan. Continue to cook for 7 minutes or until browned on each side. The frittata can be served hot or cold.

The omelet is ready when browned on both sides.

Frittata is a great appetizer and can be prepared the day before, refrigerated and then cut into 2-inch squares and served cold.

Some of the artichokes in Italy are a beautiful purple color and have an exquisite taste. Often, they are also used raw in a salad.

In questo mondo non cé altro che mangiare bene e star contento.
(In this world, nothing is as important as eating well and being happy.)

FRITTATA DI CARCIOFI
Artichoke Frittata

10 small artichokes (found in specialty stores)
½ onion
¼ cup olive oil
5 large eggs
1 teaspoon parsley, freshly chopped
salt and pepper

Remove the tough outer leaves on the artichokes. Wash and thinly slice the artichokes. Finely chop the onion.

In a 10-inch nonstick skillet, heat the olive oil and add the onions and artichokes. Sauté over low heat for 12 minutes or until the artichokes are tender.

In a medium bowl, beat the eggs and mix in the parsley, salt and pepper. Add the artichokes to the egg mixture and mix well. Pour the egg and artichoke mixture into the skillet and cook for 5 minutes or until the frittata is browned on the bottom. Gently slide the frittata onto a flat plate, put the pan over the dish and turn the frittata upside down, back into the pan. Continue to cook for 5 minutes or until golden brown on both sides.

Place the frittata on a serving dish and slice into quarters.

 MEDIUM

INSALATE SALADS

Insalate, or salads, are always served after the *secondo* and before the cheese and fruit in traditional Tuscan households. A typical Tuscan salad can be made from lettuce or arugula and artichokes or other fresh vegetables. Some salads are topped with mozzarella or pecorino cheese. The dressing is usually a whisked combination of wine vinegar, olive oil, pepper and salt. A hint of mustard is sometimes added for a provocative, tangy taste.

Excellent as a summer starter
or for lunch.

INSALATA ESTIVA CON MOZZARELLA
Summer Salad with Fresh Mozzarella

3 medium tomatoes (preferably
   San Marziano or roma)
5 fresh basil sprigs
½ pound fresh mozzarella
½ cup olive oil
2 tablespoons balsamic vinegar
   salt and pepper

Wash and slice the tomatoes. Wash the basil and separate the
leaves. Slice the mozzarella. Arrange and alternate the sliced
tomatoes, mozzarella and basil leaves on a platter. Chill for about
30 minutes. Combine the olive oil, vinegar, salt and pepper and
whisk. Pour over the salad and serve.

162

FAGIOLI, CIPOLLA E POMODORO
Bean, Onion and Tomato Salad

2   15-ounce cans cannellini beans or
    2 cups cooked cranberry beans
1   small red onion, chopped
1   celery stalk, chopped
2   tomatoes (preferably roma)
3   basil leaves, chopped
¼   cup extra virgin olive oil
1   tablespoon balsamic vinegar
    salt and pepper

Drain and rinse the cannellini beans. Finely chop the onion and celery. Coarsely chop the tomatoes. Chop the basil and put it aside.

In a large bowl, combine the cannellini beans, onion, celery and tomatoes. In a smaller bowl, combine the olive oil, vinegar, salt and pepper and mix well. Pour the mixture over the salad and garnish with the chopped basil.

This is one of those salads I can't get enough of. In the summertime in Lucca, this salad is eaten frequently as a side dish.

Fennel has a flavor like that of anise and is most tender during the months of October through March.

INSALATA DI FINOCCHI
Fennel Salad

3   fennel bulbs
½   cup olive oil
2   tablespoons balsamic vinegar
    salt and pepper

Wash and remove the tough outer leaves on the fennel bulb. Cut the bulb into thin slices.

Combine the olive oil, balsamic vinegar, salt and pepper and mix well. Pour over the fennel and serve.

INSALATA MISTA
Mixed Green Salad

3	tomatoes
1	carrot
1	fennel bulb
1	small head butter lettuce
1	small head red radicchio
15	arugula leaves
1	teaspoon dijon mustard
½	cup olive oil
1	garlic clove
3	tablespoons balsamic vinegar
	salt and pepper

Wash and dry all the vegetables. Slice the tomatoes into quarters, grate the carrot, cut the fennel into small pieces and tear the lettuce as desired.

In a small container, mix the olive oil, vinegar, mustard, garlic, salt and pepper. Allow to stand for about 1 hour. Shake well and toss with salad. Serve chilled.

This salad is a great accompaniment to almost any meal. In Lucca tuna or hardboiled eggs are often added to this salad to make a meal of it.

Coll'olio bono, si fa tutto bono!
(With good olive oil, everything is good!)

These stuffed tomatoes are wonderful either as an appetizer or as a light lunch. Using fresh tomatoes during the summer make this recipe even more flavorful.

Pomodori Farciti
Stuffed Tomatoes

6	medium tomatoes (not too ripe)
⅔	cup bread crumbs
¼	cup wine vinegar
6	anchovies, packed in oil
2	tablespoons capers
1½	tablespoons parsley, freshly chopped
	salt
6	basil leaves
½	cup extra virgin olive oil

Wash the tomatoes and pat them dry. Slice the tops off and remove a small portion of the inside of each tomato (about a teaspoon and a half). Also remove the seeds.

Place the bread crumbs in a small bowl, add the vinegar and allow to sit for 5 minutes. Squeeze all the excess vinegar from the bread crumbs and set them aside.

Chop and mash the anchovies and capers together. Add the parsley and salt and mix well. Add the bread crumbs and olive oil and mix well with a fork.

Take a heaping teaspoon of the mixture and fill the inside of each tomato. Garnish with a basil leaf.

Refrigerate the tomatoes for about a ½ hour. Before serving, drizzle each tomato with extra virgin olive oil.

MEDIUM

Insalata di Rucola, Radicchio e Parmigiano
Arugula, Radicchio and Shaved Parmesan Salad

1	small head red radicchio
10	ounces arugula leaves
½	cup shaved Parmesan cheese
¼	cup olive oil
1	tablespoon balsamic vinegar
	salt and freshly ground pepper

Wash and thoroughly dry the radicchio and arugula leaves. Tear the larger leaves into smaller pieces.

In a small bowl, add the olive oil, balsamic vinegar and salt and whisk well.

Arrange the salad in a mixing bowl, pour the salad dressing over the salad and sprinkle with the shaved Parmesan cheese and freshly ground pepper.

The distinct flavor of arugula gives this salad a unique taste.

DOLCI DESSERTS

I dolci literally means "the sweets." No matter how delicious a meal has been, the guests always have high expectations for the dessert. Italian desserts are not necessarily terribly sweet. Plain cakes topped with fruit or an Italian cream, or biscotti dipped in vin santo followed by fragrant espresso and plenty of lively conversation are the typical ending for Tuscan evenings at a restaurant or at home among family and friends.

This dessert is truly divine and not that difficult to make.

Mangiamo! tanto in questo mondo ci siam per le spese.
(Let's eat! In this world we count for so little.)

ZUCCOTTO
Frozen Cream Cake

1 cube sweet butter
1 cup almonds, chopped
1 teaspoon vanilla extract
2 pints whipped cream
½ cup mescolanza (mixture of sweet liqueurs—for instance, sweet marsala, sweet vermouth, frangelico)
½ cup espresso coffee
2 boxes ladyfinger cookies

Allow the butter to soften. Beat the butter on high speed for 5 minutes or until creamy. Add the chopped almonds and vanilla. Lightly whip cream. Mix well. In a medium-sized bowl, add the liqueurs and espresso. Crumble 1 box of ladyfingers. Add 2 tablespoons of the liqueurs to the crumbled cookies and add to the mixture. Mix well.

In a 12-inch-diameter plastic bowl 6 inches deep, place a piece of waxed paper large enough to cover the inside. One by one, gently dip the ladyfingers into the liqueurs and place them all around the bottom and the sides of the bowl. Add the whipped cream mixture. Cover the top with plastic wrap and freeze for approximately 6 hours.

Remove the bowl from the freezer 15 minutes before serving, place a dish over the bowl and turn upside down. Remove the waxed paper. Slice and serve.

The zuccotto should have the consistency of ice cream.

 MEDIUM

FRITTELLE DI RISO
Rice Fritters

2   cups water
1   cup arborio rice
4   eggs
½   cup sugar
3   tablespoons butter
1   teaspoon vanilla extract
1   tablespoon lemon rind
1   tablespoon marsala wine
1   cup flour
2   cups light vegetable oil
2   tablespoons powdered sugar

Cook the rice in 2 cups of boiling water for 20 minutes and drain well. Separate the eggs, beat the whites in a separate bowl and set them aside. Beat the egg yolks with the sugar for 3 to 4 minutes. Add the softened butter and continue to beat. Add the vanilla extract, lemon rind and marsala. When all the flour has been added, add the cooked rice and mix well. Add the egg whites to the rice mixture and mix well with a wooden spoon.

Heat the vegetable oil in a deep frying pan. Drop a round tablespoon of the batter into the oil and deep-fry it until it is golden brown. Place the cooked rice fritters on paper towels to soak up excess oil. Sprinkle them with the powdered sugar and serve warm.

MEDIUM

These frittelle typically are served on St. Joseph's Day, March 19, a Lucca tradition.

Scarpaccia is a very thin zucchini cake traditionally made only in Viareggio. About 1 inch high, scarpaccia is not very sweet but has an excellent flavor, especially when made with small, home-grown zucchini.

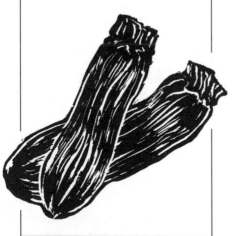

SCARPACCIA
Viareggio-Style Zucchini Cake

5	small zucchini
	salt
3	eggs
½	cup sugar
3	tablespoons butter
1	teaspoon vanilla
¾	cup flour

Slice the zucchini into very thin rounds. Place the pieces on a large dish and sprinkle them with salt. Allow them to stand for about 30 minutes to rid them of excess liquid. Drain the zucchini well and dry.

In a bowl, combine the eggs and sugar and beat them until creamy. Add 2 tablespoons of the softened butter and vanilla and continue to beat for 3 more minutes. Add about ¾ cup of the flour and continue to mix. The consistency should be that of a thin batter. More flour may be needed. Add the sliced zucchini and mix with a wooden spoon.

The best pan I have ever used to make this is a cast-iron one, 9 inches by 13 inches. Any heavy pan that can be placed in the oven will work. Butter the bottom and sides of the pan. Pour the batter into the pan and bake at 375 degrees for about 50 minutes. Allow to cool. Then turn out onto a serving dish.

EASY

MANTOVANA
Simple Yellow Cake

1 egg
¾ cup sugar
1 lemon rind, grated
3 egg yolks
1 cup flour
1 cube butter, softened
⅔ cup toasted almonds, slivered

Beat the whole egg with the sugar for 3 minutes on medium speed. Add the lemon rind and the egg yolks one by one and continue to beat until the batter is smooth and creamy. Gradually add the sifted flour and continue to beat on medium speed. Add the butter and beat for 3 more minutes on high speed.

Pour the batter into a buttered, 10-inch glass pie dish and sprinkle the almonds on top.

Bake for 40 to 45 minutes at 350 degrees or until a toothpick inserted into the center of the cake comes out dry.

This is one of my favorite afternoon snack cakes. A slice of Mantovana and an espresso go great together.

A scoop of vanilla ice cream or a tablespoon of fresh whipped cream is ideal on this cake.

DOLCE DI MELE
Apple Cake

4	cups apples, sliced
2	cups sugar
2	cups flour
1½	teaspoons baking soda
½	teaspoon salt
1½	teaspoons cinnamon
2	eggs
2	teaspoons vanilla extract
¾	cup light vegetable oil
1	cup walnuts, chopped

Wash, peel and core the apples. Slice apples thinly and combine with the sugar in a large bowl. Allow to sit for about 10 minutes.

Sift the flour together with the baking soda, salt and cinnamon. Beat the eggs. Pour the flour and vanilla extract over the apples and mix well with a spoon. Pour the eggs, oil and walnuts and mix well with a wooden spoon. Butter a 9-by-13-inch baking dish and pour the batter evenly inside of a pan. Bake at 350 degrees for 50 to 55 minutes.

BISCOTTI DI MIA NONNA
My Grandmother's Cookies

2 cups flour
2 teaspoons baking powder
6 eggs
2 cups sugar
1 cube butter, melted
½ cup mixed sweet cordials (for instance,
   sweet marsala, sweet vermouth, frangelico)
1½ cups toasted almonds, slivered
   flour as needed

Sift 2 cups of flour and baking powder. Set aside.

Beat the eggs. Then gradually add the sugar and continue to beat
on medium speed until all the sugar has been added and the
mixture is creamy. Add butter. Add the sweet cordials and
almonds and continue to beat for about a minute.

Slowly add the flour and baking powder and continue to beat
until the mixture resembles a thick dough. When the dough
becomes too thick to beat, knead by hand and continue to add
the flour until the dough is sticky, but pliable.

Flour a pastry board. Cut about ¼ of the dough and roll it into a
2-by-10-inch roll. Flatten the roll with your hands so that the roll is
about 1 inch thick. Repeat this process with the remaining dough.
Butter 2 cookie sheets and gently place the cookie dough rolls on
the sheets. Bake in the oven at 375 degrees for 25 minutes.

Remove the cookie rolls from the oven, place on a cutting board
and cut into about 1-inch diagonal cookies. Return to the oven
and bake until golden brown on each side. The cookies may need
to be turned once to achieve the desired golden color.

These cookies taste wonderful
when dipped in vin santo, a
sweet after-dinner wine made in
Tuscany. Biscotti are frequently
served in many of the Lucchese
restaurants after a meal. These
cookies will keep for a month or
more if properly stored in an
air-tight cookie jar.

 MEDIUM

TORTA COI BECCHI
Sweet Vegetable Pie

½ pound Swiss chard
2 tablespoons butter
2 tablespoons parsley, freshly chopped
3 thick slices of panettone bread
   or 15 ladyfingers
½ cup milk
3 eggs
¾ cup sugar
½ cup raisins
½ cup pine nuts
1 teaspoon salt
¼ cup mixed sweet cordials (for instance,
   sweet marsala, sweet vermouth, frangelico)

Clean the Swiss chard and remove and dispose of the large stalks.
Bring a large pot of water to a boil, add the Swiss chard and cook until
it is tender (approximately 15 minutes). When the chard is cooked,
drain well and squeeze out any excess water. Chop it finely.

In a medium pan, heat the butter over medium heat, add the
chopped chard and parsley and sauté for 5 minutes. Remove from
the heat and set aside.

Soak the panettone in the milk. Then squeeze it to remove all the
excess milk from the bread. If using ladyfingers, soak these in
milk and repeat the process.

In a large bowl, add the eggs and sugar and whisk well. Add the
Swiss chard, panettone, raisins, pine nuts, salt and cordials and
mix well. The mixture should not be liquid. If it is, add additional
panettone or ladyfingers. Prepare the torta crust, add the filling
and cook as described on page 177.

MEDIUM

PIE CRUST FOR TORTA

1½   cubes butter
1¼   cup sugar
 1   teaspoon baking powder
 ¼   cup mixed sweet cordials (for instance,
     sweet marsala, sweet vermouth, frangelico)
2½   cups flour

Melt the butter. In a large bowl, add the melted butter and sugar
and beat at medium speed for 5 minutes or until the texture is
creamy. Add the cordials and continue to beat for 2 more minutes.
Add the baking powder to the flour and gradually add the flour to
the mix, beating constantly. The mixture should be a little sticky.
If necessary, add a little more flour. Keep in mind that the more
flour you add, the tougher the dough becomes.

Butter a 10-inch baking dish and dust it with flour. Roll out the
dough somewhat thinly to cover the dish, add the filling and
make a fluted border. Cook in a preheated oven at 350 degrees for
55 minutes or until the crust is golden brown.

 MEDIUM

This recipe makes approximately
18 two-inch cream puffs.

BIGNE RIPIENI
Small Cream Puffs

    1   cup water
    1   cube butter
        pinch of salt
    1   cup flour
    4   eggs
    ½   cup powdered sugar
    3   cups Italian cream filling (see page
        179 for recipe)

Bring the water to a boil. Add the butter. When the butter has
melted, lower the heat and add the flour and salt and mix well for
about 2 minutes. Remove from the heat and allow to cool for
about 10 minutes.

When the mixture has cooled, add 1 egg at a time, mixing well
after each egg.

On a cookie sheet, drop tablespoons of the mixture until there are
about 18 drops on the sheet. Preheat the oven to 375 degrees and
bake for 50 to 55 minutes or until golden brown.

Cut each cream puff in half, add a spoonful of Italian cream and
sprinkle with powdered sugar.

CREMA ITALIANA
Italian Cream

  3   egg yolks
  ¾   cup sugar
  1   lemon rind, grated
  2½   tablespoons flour
  ¼   cup of sweet cordials (for instance, sweet
       marsala, sweet vermouth, frangelico)
  2   cups milk

Beat the egg yolks and sugar on medium speed for 4 minutes,
add the lemon rind and flour and continue to beat for 4 more
minutes. Add the cordials and milk and beat for 2 more minutes.

Place the mixture in a medium-sized pot on medium heat.
Constantly stir the mixture, allowing it to come to a boil. As the
mixture thickens, remove it from the heat and allow it to cool.

EASY

You can make easy and
wonderful desserts with this
cream, such as pan di spagna
cake or ladyfingers layered with
cream and drizzled with liqueurs
and cream. Serve with shaved
fresh chocolate.

PESCHE RIPIENE
Amaretto-Stuffed Peaches

    6   firm peaches
   ¼   cup blanched almonds
    1   egg yolk
   ½   cup sugar
   12   amaretto cookies
   ¼   cup amaretto liqueur
    1   tablespoon butter

Wash, dry and halve the peaches. Remove the pits and scoop out a tablespoon of the peach pulp from each half.

In a food processor, add the peach pulp, almonds, egg yolk, sugar, amaretto cookies and liqueur. Blend until well pureed.

Butter the bottom of a large baking dish. Place a tablespoon full of the mixture into each peach half and arrange in a baking dish in a single layer. Bake at 350 degrees for 25 minutes.

Allow to stand 20 minutes or chill for 1 hour before serving.

The best time to make this dessert is in the summer, when peaches are in season. It is quick, easy and wonderful to eat.

VARIATION
Add a tablespoon of whipped cream to each half and top with an amaretto cookie.

Pan di Spagna
Italian-Style Sponge Cake

6 eggs
1 cup sugar
1 teaspoon vanilla
1¼ cups flour
    pinch of salt
2 teaspoons baking powder
1 teaspoon butter

Separate the egg yolks and whites. Beat the egg yolks on medium speed until they are creamy. Gradually add sugar and continue to beat until mixture is creamy. Add vanilla, flour, salt and baking powder. Continue to beat on medium speed for 5 more minutes.

Beat egg whites until fluffy. Then fold them into the cake mixture.

Preheat oven to 350 degrees. Butter a 9-by-12-inch cake pan and cook for 40 minutes at 350 degrees.

Allow to cool, and remove from pan.

This cake typically is used as sponge cake to be served with macedonia or Italian cream. Slice the cake and add macedonia with some vanilla ice cream and you have a delicious and elegant dessert.

This is an easy, light dessert commonly served in many restaurants in Italy.

CREM CARAMEL
Custard

<table>
<tr><td>3</td><td>eggs</td></tr>
<tr><td>1½</td><td>cups milk</td></tr>
<tr><td>1</td><td>teaspoon vanilla</td></tr>
<tr><td>1</td><td>tablespoon rum</td></tr>
<tr><td>⅓</td><td>cup sugar</td></tr>
</table>

Combine the eggs, milk, vanilla and rum and beat. Make sure the ingredients are well combined but not foamy.

In a saucepan, cook the sugar over medium heat. Do not stir until the sugar begins to melt. Gently shake the saucepan so that the sugar does not burn. Reduce the heat to low and continue to cook until the sugar has browned, stirring frequently. Pour the sugar mixture into a soufflé pan so that the bottom of the pan is well coated with the sugar mixture. Allow it to stand for 8 minutes before adding the custard mixture.

Place a 3½-cup soufflé dish in a large pan on an oven rack. Pour the custard mixture into the dish. Gently add boiling water into the larger pan to a depth of about 1 inch so that the soufflé dish is submerged in the larger pan with the water.

Cook for 50 minutes at 350 degrees or until a knife inserted into the middle of the custard comes out clean.

Remove from the larger saucepan and loosen the crem caramel by inserting a knife around the edge of the mold. While it is still warm, turn it out onto a serving plate. Allow it to cool. Refrigerate for 1 hour before serving.

 MEDIUM

TORTA DI CASTAGNE
Tuscan Chestnut Cake

1   rosemary sprig
2   tablespoons walnuts, chopped
1   pound chestnut flour
4   tablespoons olive oil
    pinch of salt
2   cups water

Chop the rosemary and set it aside. Coarsely chop the walnuts and set them aside.

In a large mixing bowl, place the chestnut flour, 2 tablespoons of olive oil and salt and mix the ingredients thoroughly. Gradually add the water, stirring continuously. The consistency of the batter should resemble that of a thin pancake batter.

Coat a 12-inch ovenproof pan with 1 tablespoon of olive oil. Pour in the batter and sprinkle the rosemary and walnuts evenly over the top of the cake. Drizzle evenly with the remaining olive oil.

Preheat the oven to 375 degrees. Bake for 50 minutes. This chestnut cake will be only about 1 inch high and should be crusty on the top and moist on the inside.

Remove it from the pan and place it on a serving dish.

 MEDIUM

Typical of the Tuscany region, torta di castagne usually is made in autumn and early winter, when the chestnut flour has been freshly ground.

CENCI
Fried Tuscan Pastries

2½ cups flour
2 eggs
6 tablespoons sugar
   light olive oil
2 tablespoons sweet marsala wine
1 lemon rind, grated
¼ cup powdered sugar

Place the flour in a bowl and add the eggs, sugar, 3 tablespoons
of olive oil, marsala wine and lemon rind. Beat for 3 minutes
at high speed.

Thoroughly mix the ingredients with your hands. Then knead the
dough until it is smooth and elastic. The dough should be rolled
into a very thin sheet. Remember, the thinner the better. Use a
fluted pastry wheel and cut the dough into thin strips about
6 inches long and ½ inch wide. Tie each strip into a knot or a bow.

In a large frying pan, heat the oil and deep-fry the cenci until it is
golden brown on each side. Drain on paper towels and sift the
powdered sugar over them.

MEDIUM

MACEDONIA
Mixed Fresh Fruit

2   peaches
1   pear
1   nectarine
10 cherries, pitted
½   cup grapes
1   apple
1   kiwi
1   orange
1   banana
½   cup sugar
1   lemon, juice only
¾   cup mixed sweet cordials (for instance,
    sweet marsala, sweet vermouth, frangelica)

Peel, slice and dice the fruit and place it in a serving bowl.
Add the sugar, lemon juice and mixed cordials. Mix well and
refrigerate for 2 hours before serving.

Macedonia is a refreshing way
to end a meal and a very popular
dessert during the summer in
Italy. It also can be topped with
fresh cream or served over a slice
of sponge cake, such as pan di
spagna.

FORMAGGI CHEESES

Italy is famous for the high quality of its cheese, so it is little wonder that traditional Tuscan meals feature a colorful cheese and fruit platter. Italians believe that cheese and fruit cleanse the palate. The cheeses listed in this section are from all regions of Italy.

The large variety of cheeses available in Italy is reflected in the number of different cheeses used in Italian cooking. Cheese in Italy is an indispensable ingredient for many recipes, from pasta dishes and pizzas to desserts.

Cheese is as much a part of an Italian table as pasta, olive oil and wine.

Il pan fa carne, il vin fa sangue, e 'l cacio mette forza nelle gambe.
(Bread gives life, wine makes blood and cheese gives strength.)

ASIAGO

This semi hard cheese is made with cow's milk and is low in fat. It usually is eaten when it is about 6 months old; however, it can be aged, grated and used for cooking. The unmatured cheese has a delicate taste. The more asiago is aged, the more flavorful it becomes.

CACIOTTA TOSCANA

Caciotta can be made from an endless variety of goat's, cow's and sheep's milk. A relatively mild-flavored cheese, it can be eaten new or aged. Some of the best casciotta comes from San Gimignano and Maremma.

FONTINA

Made with cow's milk, this cheese is a full-fat, dry-salted cheese that generally is matured for about 100 days. Fontina is a good table cheese and can be used in cooking.

GORGONZOLA

This is Italy's version of blue cheese. It is even tastier when soft, almost like a brie.

MASCARPONE

Very similar to a sweet cream cheese, mascarpone usually is used in desserts. It also is used in some pasta sauce recipes.

MOZZARELLA

Mozzarella in Italy is quite different from what we are accustomed to in America. The finest mozzarella is made from the milk of water buffaloes and literally is called mozzarella di bufalo. It also can be made from cow's milk. This is a white cheese that is very fresh and is packaged in its own whey and water. A very mild cheese, mozzarella typically is round or pear shaped. This type of mozzarella usually is found only at specialty stores.

PARMIGIANO

Parmigiano (Parmesan) is one of the finest cheeses in the world and has been produced in Italy for centuries. Made from cow's milk, parmigiano is aged for at least 2 years, giving it a strong flavor. It is the cheese used most widely with pasta and is usually freshly grated for best results. Parmigiano is a wonderful cheese to serve with fresh fruit at the end of a meal.

PECORINO

Pecorino cheese probably is as popular in Italy as parmigiano is. This cheese is particularly strong and is made with ewe's milk. Pecorino can be grated and served on pastas or eaten at the end of a meal with fruit. Fresh pecorino, which is aged only several months, usually is eaten by the slice. The more mature cheese is harder, with a stronger flavor, and usually is served grated.

PROVOLONE

This cheese is also made from cow's milk. Provolone is straw colored and comes in three varieties: mild, strong and smoked. The longer the cheese is aged, the stronger the flavor becomes.

RICOTTA

A creamy cheese, ricotta is made from the discarded whey of other cheeses. In Italy, ricotta usually is made from the whey of ewe's milk, which gives it a rich taste. Ricotta is used in many pasta dishes and some dessert dishes. A mild cheese, ricotta contains no salt.

TALEGGIO

This cheese originated in Lombardy, at the foot of the Alps. Taleggio is made with cow's milk and is dry salted. This soft cheese is completely ripe after about 40 days and has a subtle, aromatic taste that strengthens with age. The rind is soft and very thin.

VINI WINES

No Italian meal would be complete without wine to enhance the flavor of the food.

ASTI SPUMANTE

Made from the muscat grape. Luscious, sweet, smooth, with intense, exotic fruit flavors. Good with desserts.

BARBARESCO

A flavorful, full, robust, yet velvety red wine. A wonderful partner when served with roast or broiled meats.

BAROLO

A full, robust red wine. Barolo is a great accompaniment to roasts, game and braised meats.

CABERNET SAUVIGNON

California's best red grape. Dry, deeply colored, rich and tannic. Good with beef, lamb and pastas.

CHARDONNAY

California's top white grape. Ranges from dry, simple unoaked versions to rich oaky, spicey and buttery wines. Some are lively, well balanced and flavorful. Sweeter chardonnays can be served with salads, chicken and cold meats. Dry chardonnays go well with shellfish, seafood, pastas and vegetables and work well as aperitifs or summer afternoon sippers.

CHENIN BLANC

Two styles exist: dry or slightly off dry and light. Sweet chenin blanc with good acidity is best consumed young and fresh. Dry chenin blanc often is served with light fish, chicken, pork and liver.

CHIANTI CLASSICO

A ruby garnet-colored wine with a well-balanced flavor. Dry, slightly tannic, becoming more refined and mellow as it ages. This wine easily can accompany all courses.

DOLCETTO

Red medium-bodied, fruity fresh wine. The so-called "Beaujolais of Piemonte." Often a first-course wine, it is an easy-drinking wine with simple foods. Great with grilled meats, pastas, risotto and cheeses.

Pan d'un giorno,
vin d'un anno.
(Fresh bread, aged wine)

FRASCATI

Made from trebbiano, malvosia and other grapes from Rome. Fragrant and delicate, this is the white wine of everyone's Roman memories. Excellent with mild-flavored dishes.

GEWÜRZTRAMINER

Grape is usually sweet with a hint of spiciness in aroma and flavor. Good with fresh fruit or fruit salads or just to sip.

GRIGNOLINO

A ruby red wine with a delicate aroma and a dry, slightly tannic flavor. An excellent wine with antipasto and soups.

MERLOT

Tough and firm as cabernet. Age accentuates the grape's soft, plummy fruit and alluring texture. Italian merlots tend to be a bit more tannic than those from California but have the same soft fruit. Good with roasted game, roasted meats and grilled or skewered meats. Especially good with lamb, steak, duck, goose and rabbit.

MONTEPULCIANO D'ABRUZZO

A bright ruby red wine. A dry, mellow flavor, lively and tannic. Excellent with meat, pasta dishes, omelets, and game.

MUSCAT CANELLI

Light, spicy, faintly exotic flavors. Lightly sweet to very sweet when harvested late. Great with peaches, pears, strawberries and desserts.

ORVIETO

Lightly fruity, fresh, usually fully dry. Dry orvietos can be used exactly as frascati—the sweet wine makes a very pleasant aperitif. Excellent for pastas with cream sauces, seafood, rabbit or salads with light vinaigrette.

Chi vendemmia troppo presto, non fa vino fa l'agresto.
(Those who harvest their grapes too soon, do not make good wine.)

193

Petite Sirah

Dark, hefty, richly textured reds that have flavors of black raspberries and some of the peppery character of Rhone reds. Good with grilled steak, meat or game, stews and savory cheeses.

Pinot Noir

Brick colored, fruitier at a younger age. Some of the cherry-colored pinots have an intense flavor without the tannin of their more exalted brothers. Good with grilled roast or chicken, salmon, roast pork and mild cheeses.

Riesling (Johannisberg or White)

Off dry to lightly sweet to very sweet when harvested late. These wines are lovely, fragrant, flowery and drinkable when young. Good on their own or with fresh fruit or light desserts. Drink dry riesling with chicken or light fish, such as sea bass, trout and salmon. Good aperitif.

Sauvignon Blanc (Fumé Blanc)

Often described as dry, crisp, white barreled, fermented or aged for a time in oak. Most are dry but have some residual sugar and a well-balanced hint of citrus. Good as a pleasant aperitif but best as a middleweight dinner wine for rich fish or shellfish, fowl or white meats.

Soave

A light wine with an uncomplicated flavor. Good as an aperitif or with light, mildly flavored foods. Best with antipasti and light pastas.

Vernaccia di San Gimignano

Light, clean, with small fruit flavors. Sometimes barrel-aged specimens exhibit oaky or vanilla overtones with an almond character. Good with gnocchi, mushrooms and seafood broiled or poached with light sauces.

Zinfandel

The most American of reds, robustly fruity with flavors reminiscent of raspberries. Some versions are fairly tannic. Good with roasted meats, sausages and cold meats. Very drinkable for complete meal.

Il vino e' il secondo pane.
(Wine is the second bread.)

GLOSSARY
OF ITALIAN
TERMS

Acciughe: Anchovies. Like Mediterranean sardines, anchovies are rather small. They usually are preserved in salt, washed and boned with heads removed before use. Fillets are cleaned and preserved in olive oil, ready for use.

Al dente: Literally means "to the tooth." This term generally is used in reference to the way pasta is cooked. In Italy, pasta is always cooked a bit firm to the bite, or *al dente*.

Antipasto: A course served before the pasta or soup dish. At times, takes the place of the first course.

Arborio rice: A plump oval-shaped rice, shorter and rounder than American rice.

Baccalà: Codfish preserved in salt. Baccalà requires soaking under cold water for a day before cooking to soften the fish and also to remove the salty taste.

Basilico: Basil. A distinctively aromatic herb, basil is used in light, summery Italian dishes and is one of the main ingredients of pesto.

Biscotti: Hard-textured cookies, usually made with almonds and not very sweet. These cookies are best when dipped in sweet wine or coffee.

Bollito: Literally means "boiled." Bollito is made up of different meats, such as beef, chicken or even sausages. When fresh broth is made, the meat for the soup is eaten as a second course, served with boiled potatoes.

Braciole: Wide, very thin slice of beef, without bone.

Brodo: Broth. In Italy, fresh broth is made weekly, sometimes even more frequently. It generally is made from chicken and served with pastina, or small noodles, as a first course. The boiled chicken meat is then served as the second course.

Cacciucco: Fish stew is a substantial dish served as a main course. Generally made with a wide variety of seafood, including fresh clams, mussels, crabs and prawns, in a light tomato sauce. It is served over toasted garlic bread.

Calamari: Small squid. These fish are excellent when deep fried or sautéed.

Cannelloni: Tube type of pasta, filled with either meat or ricotta and baked in an oven.

Capperi: Capers, pickled and tart, are used in a variety of Italian dishes, most often on pizza.

Cartoccio: An Italian term for meat or fish wrapped in paper. It indicates a way to cook different foods. More common today to use aluminum foil.

Ceci: Garbanzo beans. Used either dried or canned.

Cenci: Tuscan pastries made with egg, flour and sweet cordials. They are thinly rolled out, cut and tied into knots or bows, then lightly fried and sprinkled with powdered sugar.

Costolette: Can be either a lamb chop, veal chop or pork chop.

Crostini: A common type of antipasto in Italian cuisine, crostini consists of small, toasted bread or polenta squares topped with a sauce.

Erbette: Common word used for a mixture of greens. Can include chard, mustard greens and spinach.

Farcito: Literally means "to stuff a meat." Stuffed meats are a common feature in Italy. Turkey, veal or other types of beef can be flattened, stuffed, then rolled.

Farro: A hard wheat with the husk, which should be soaked in water before being used or cooked for several hours, usually in soups.

Fennel (Finocchietto): Sweet bulb that tastes like anise and can be eaten raw in a salad or cooked.

Frittata: Resembles a flat omelet, made with eggs and vegetables.

Fritto misto: This is a typical Italian dish called "mixed fry," which can be very diverse, using various meats, such as chicken or rabbit, or a variety of mixed vegetables, such as zucchini, mushrooms or cardoon. Fish also can be prepared this way.

Gamberetti: Prawns, usually small to medium sized. Gamberi are large prawns.

Gnocchi: Small dumpling-type pasta made with potatoes, spinach and ricotta or semolina. Boiled in water and covered with a sauce.

In umido: Braising or stewing method of stove-top cooking, in which a small amount of liquid remains on the bottom of the pan.

Marsala: Can be a sweet dessert wine or a warm aromatic wine. Can be used for meats, poultry, vegetables and sweet dishes. Named after Marsala, Sicily.

Minestra: A soup with a variety of vegetables, often served with small pasta or rice.

Mozzarella: A white cheese originally made from water buffalo milk.

Olive: The best are those cured in brine, a mixture of water and salt, or those that are preserved in olive oil. The black olives have the strongest flavor.

Ossobuco: A veal or beef shank, usually cut from the middle part of the shank where the bone is smaller. The bone marrow usually is lifted out so that the delicate flavor can be savored.

Pancetta: An Italian cured meat made from the pig's belly. Pancetta resembles pork fat except for being less hard and dense and having streaks of red meat through it.

Parmigiano: A strong-flavored cheese, aged 2 years or longer. Specialty of Parma, for which it is named.

Pecorino: Cheese made from ewe's milk. Served grated on pasta dishes or served after dinner with fruit.

Peperoncino: Chili pepper. Used throughout Italy to add a spicy flavor to many dishes. Particularly good in the classic spaghetti dish spaghetti con aglio, olio e peperoncino.

Pesto: Sauce made from fresh basil, garlic, olive oil and pine nuts.

Pinzimonio: A way of displaying a variety of raw vegetables to be dipped in a mixture of olive oil, vinegar, salt and pepper.

Polenta: A coarse cornmeal, polenta is sprinkled into salted, boiling water to obtain the consistency of porridge. Polenta can be served with either a soft cheese, with melted butter or in a hearty tomato sauce full of chicken, beef and sausages.

Polpette: Small, rounded meat croquettes. They can be either oven baked or deep fried, usually coated with bread crumbs. These are best made with leftover roasted meats or poultry.

Porcini: These mushrooms are well known for their distinct flavor. In Italy, fresh porcini mushrooms are used most often. In America dried mushrooms are more widely available. Either way, they are delicious. Dried porcini should be soaked in hot water for 10 to 15 minutes. Then excess moisture should be squeezed out.

Prosciutto: A delicate, salt-cured ham. Prosciutto is very popular in Italy and very expensive. Prosciutto may be either cured or cooked. The taste is delicate and sweet.

Radicchio: Chicory. There are various types of radicchio: some red, some green and some more bitter than others. Radicchio makes a wonderful salad.

Ricotta: means "cooked twice." This is a very light cheese made from milk that has been cooked twice. In Italy, ricotta generally is made from ewe's milk, although it is also made from cow's milk.

Risotto: Arborio rice can be cooked in a broth with meat or fish or in a tomato sauce. Risotto always should be cooked *al dente*.

Salsiccia: Italian sausage. In Tuscany, this sausage usually is not very spicy and is boiled, baked or pan fried.

Saltimbocca: Literally means "jump in the mouth." Saltimbocca can be made from beef, veal or chicken. Meats are rolled over a filling or sometimes flattened, with herbs and sauces added.

Scaloppine: Very thin slices of veal. Although beef or chicken can be substituted, scaloppine typically is made with veal.

Sformato: A vegetable mold, usually made from fresh vegetables and a delicate white sauce. Very popular in the Tuscany region.

Soffritto: Blend of chopped vegetables—typically carrots, onion, celery and parsley—used to flavor soups, meats and certain sauces.

Tagliatelle: Pasta made with flour and eggs. About ⅜ inch wide and about 10 inches long.

Vin santo: A dessert wine from Tuscany.

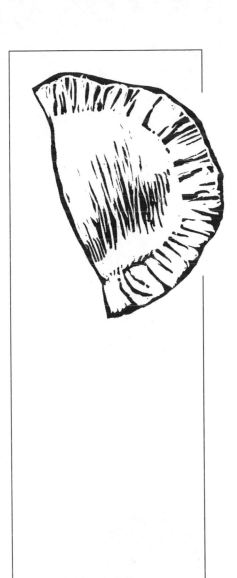

INDEX

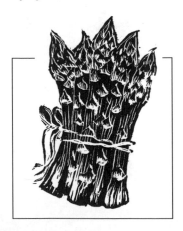

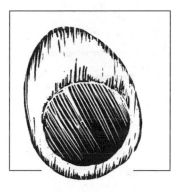